STARTER

Gregg Schroeder

COURSE CONSULTANTS

Paul Dummett

Elaine Boyd

Australia • Brazil • Mexico • Singapore • United Kingdom • United States

Scope and Sequence

Hello!
p. 4

		Words	Grammar	Phonics
1 **Hello!** p. 5		*Hello.* *Goodbye.* *Sing.* *Sit down.* *Stand up.* *Thank you.*	*Hello. How are you?* *I'm fine, thank you.* *What's your name?* *My name's Emilia.*	**a**, **b**, **c** *apple, bag, cake* VALUE Be friendly.
2 **At School** p. 11		*book, chair, crayon, desk, pencil, teacher* Numbers 1–6	*Is it a book?* *Yes, it is./* *No, it isn't.* *one pencil* *two pencil***s**	**d**, **e**, **f** *duck, egg, fish* VALUE Say thank you.
Game 1 p. 17				
3 **My Toys** p. 19		*ball, car,* *doll, robot,* *teddy bear,* *train* Colors	*What's this?* *It's a car.* *What color is it?* *It's black.*	**g**, **h**, **i** *goat, hippo, igloo* VALUE Be careful.
4 **On the Farm** p. 25		*bird, cat, cow, dog, horse, rabbit* *big, small* Numbers 7–12	*What are they?* *They're birds.* *How many birds?* *Seven.*	**j**, **k**, **l** *jam, king, lizard* VALUE Make friends.
Game 2 p. 31				
5 **I Like Food!** p. 33		*bread, chicken,* *fruit, juice, milk,* *rice, water*	*I like juice.* *I don't like bread.*	**m**, **n**, **o** *monkey, nuts, ostrich* VALUE Give and share.
6 **How Are You?** p. 39		*happy, sad, hot,* *cold, hungry, thirsty*	*I'm hungry.* *I want water.*	**p**, **q**, **r** *pink, quilt, rain* VALUE Make good choices.
Game 3 p. 45				

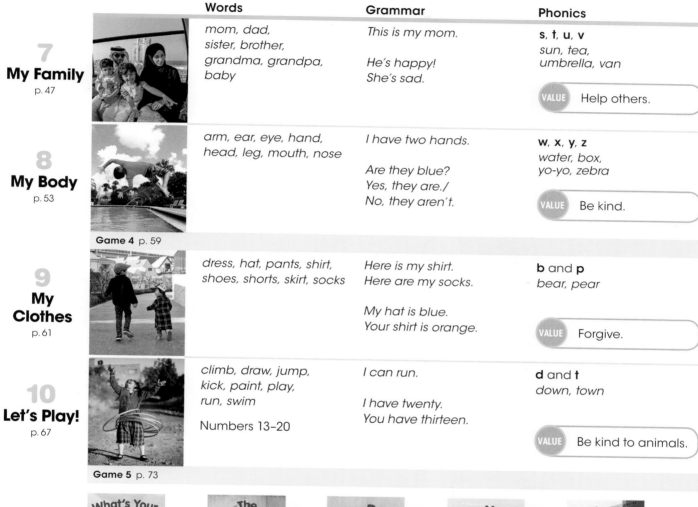

	Words	Grammar	Phonics
7 My Family p. 47	mom, dad, sister, brother, grandma, grandpa, baby	*This is my mom.* *He's happy! She's sad.*	**s**, **t**, **u**, **v** *sun, tea, umbrella, van* VALUE Help others.
8 My Body p. 53	arm, ear, eye, hand, head, leg, mouth, nose	*I have two hands.* *Are they blue? Yes, they are./ No, they aren't.*	**w**, **x**, **y**, **z** *water, box, yo-yo, zebra* VALUE Be kind.
Game 4 p. 59			
9 My Clothes p. 61	dress, hat, pants, shirt, shoes, shorts, skirt, socks	*Here is my shirt. Here are my socks.* *My hat is blue. Your shirt is orange.*	**b** and **p** *bear, pear* VALUE Forgive.
10 Let's Play! p. 67	climb, draw, jump, kick, paint, play, run, swim Numbers 13–20	*I can run.* *I have twenty. You have thirteen.*	**d** and **t** *down, town* VALUE Be kind to animals.
Game 5 p. 73			

Unit story books p. 75

Unit 1

Unit 2

Unit 3

Unit 4

Unit 5

Unit 6

Unit 7

Unit 8

Unit 9

Unit 10

Thank-you card p. 95

Hello!

1 Look and find.

Hello!

2 Trace and say.

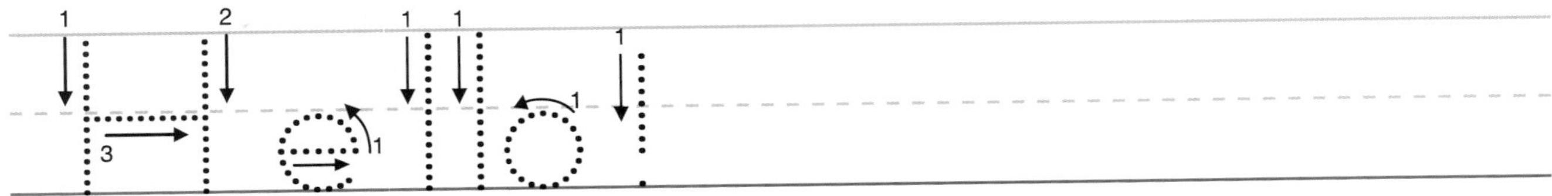

UNIT 1

Hello!

Draw a picture of you.

Words

1 Listen and point. TR: 1

Hello.

Goodbye.

Sing.

Sit down.

Stand up.

Thank you.

2 Listen and repeat. TR: 2

3 Listen and circle. TR: 3

1  

2

3 

4 

5  

6 

Grammar

1 Listen and repeat. TR: 4

2 Play and say.

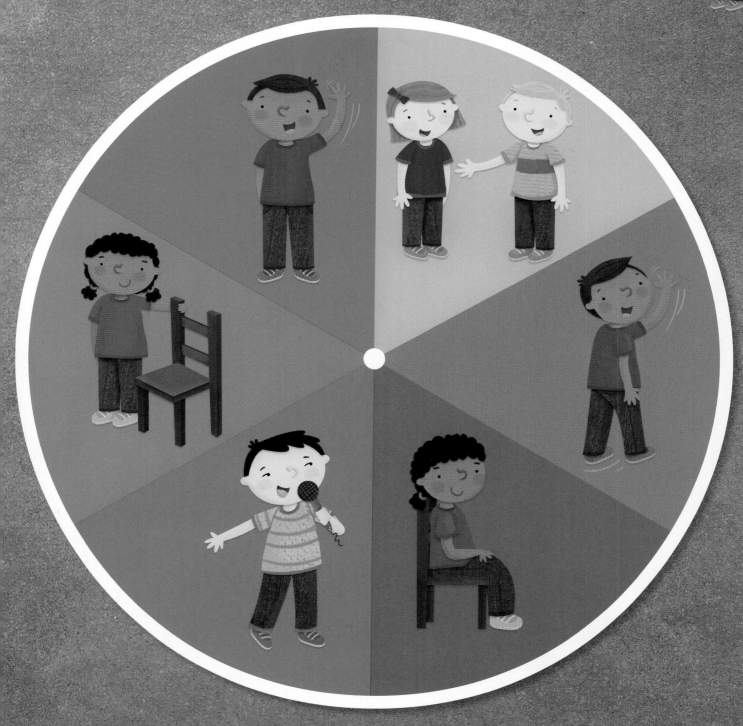

Grammar and Song

1 Listen and repeat. TR: 5

2 Listen and sing. TR: 6 and 7

Phonics

1 Listen, point, and repeat. TR: 8

2 Trace the letters

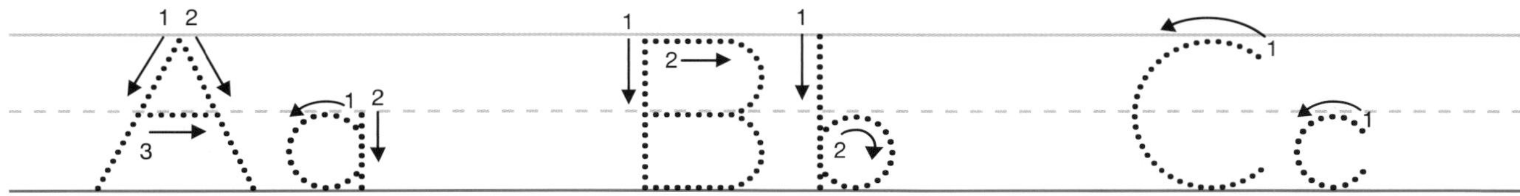

3 Listen and chant. TR: 9

4 Listen and match. TR: 10

Aa Bb Cc

LESSON 5

Video and Story

1 Watch and check (✔). Video 1

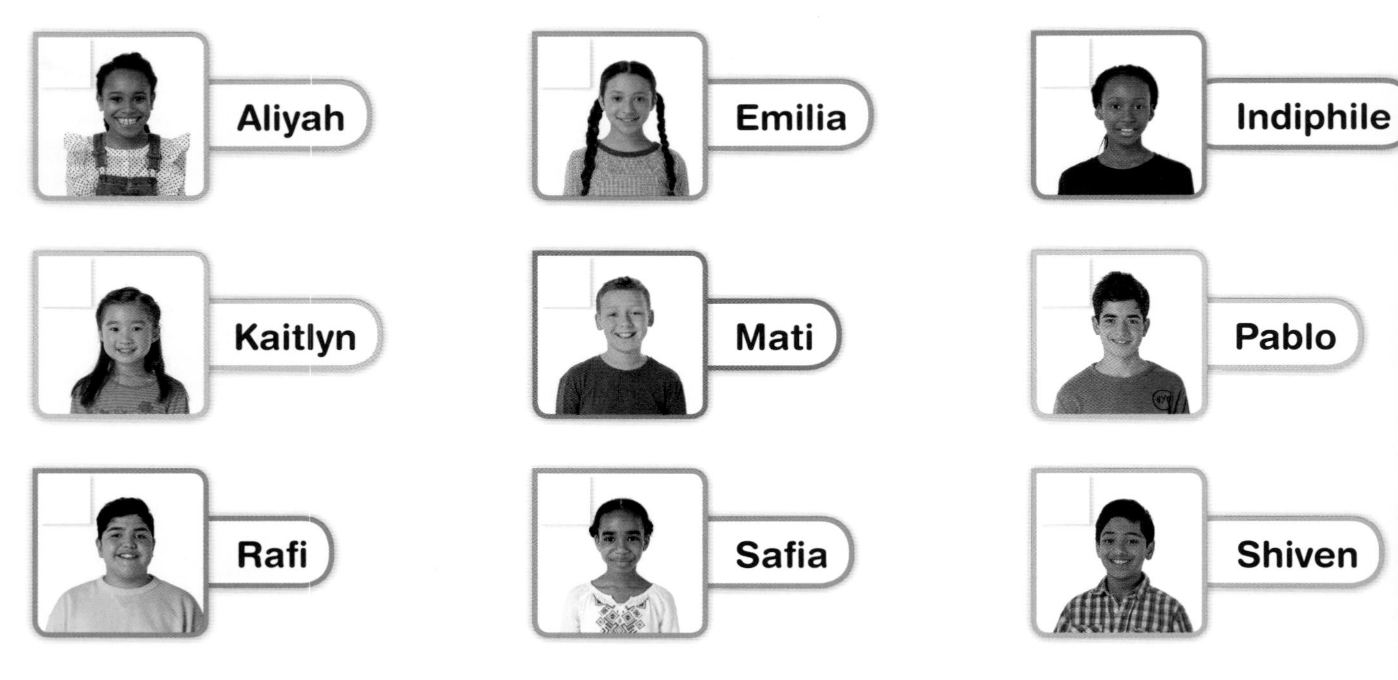

2 Read the Unit 1 story. Circle. TR: 11

VALUE **Be friendly.**
Do the Unit 1 Value activity in the Workbook.

3 Trace and say.

UNIT 2

At School

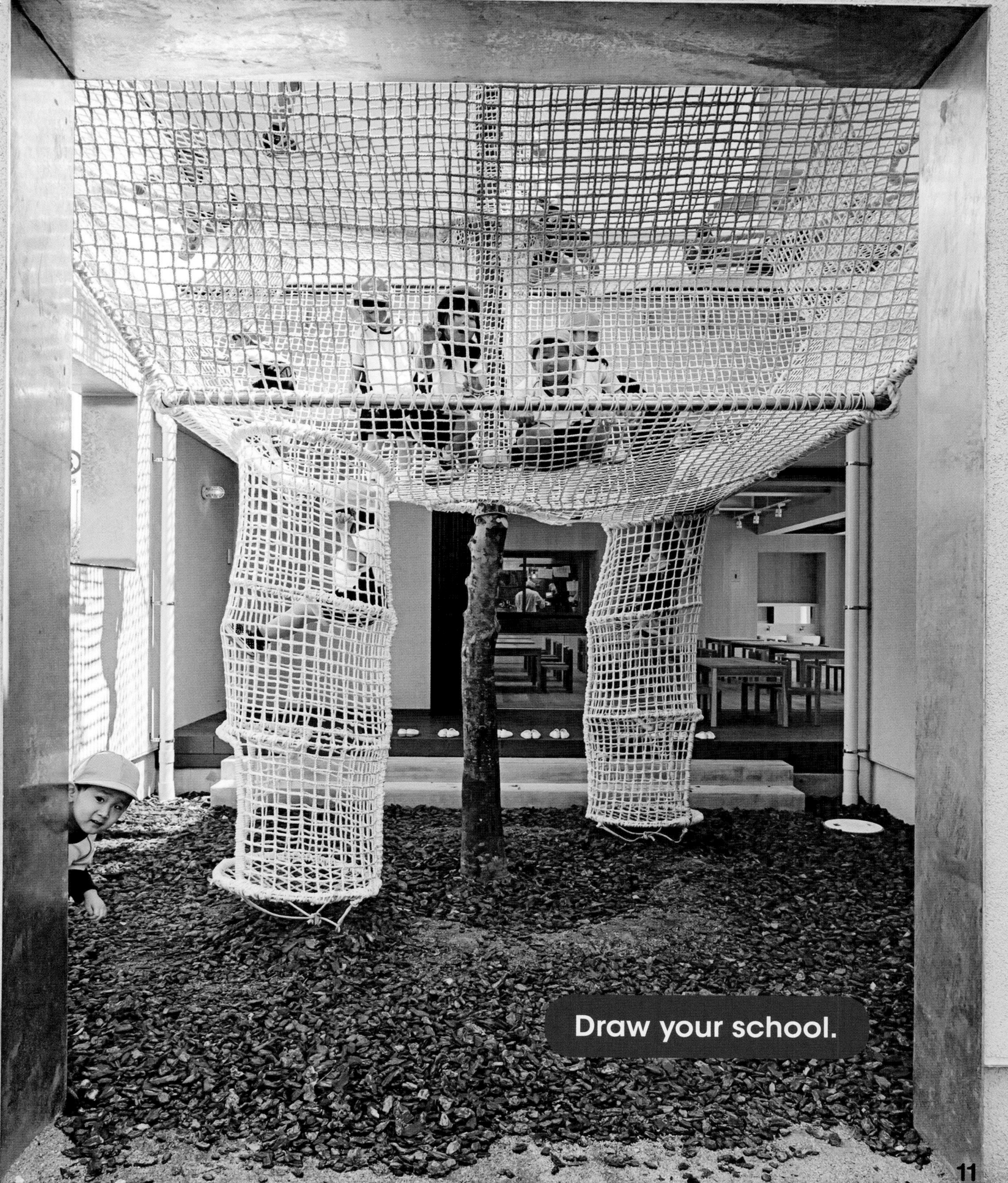

Draw your school.

LESSON 1

Words

1 Listen and point. TR: 12

book chair crayon desk pencil teacher

2 Listen and repeat. TR: 13

3 Listen and check (✓). TR: 14

Grammar

1 Listen and repeat. TR: 15

Is it a book?
Yes, it is.

Is it a crayon?
No, it isn't.

2 Play and say.

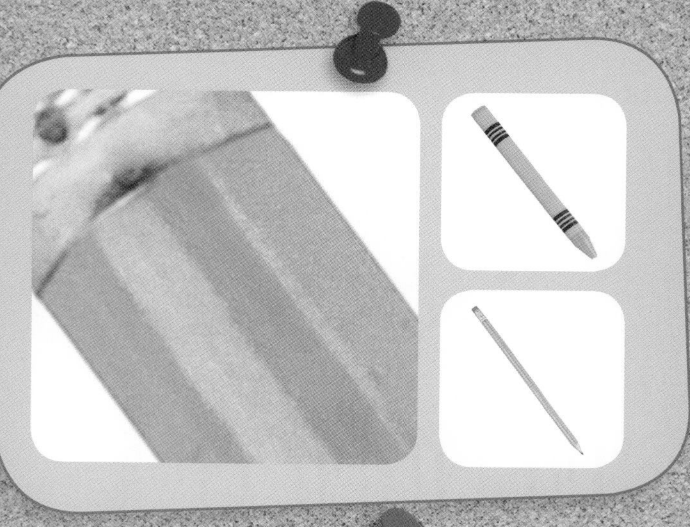

LESSON 3 Grammar and Song

1 Listen and repeat. TR: 16

2 Listen and repeat. TR: 17

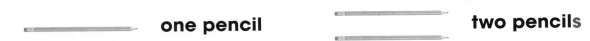

3 Listen and check (✔). Say. TR: 18

4 Listen and sing. TR: 19 and 20

Phonics

1 Listen, point, and repeat. TR: 21

2 Trace the letters.

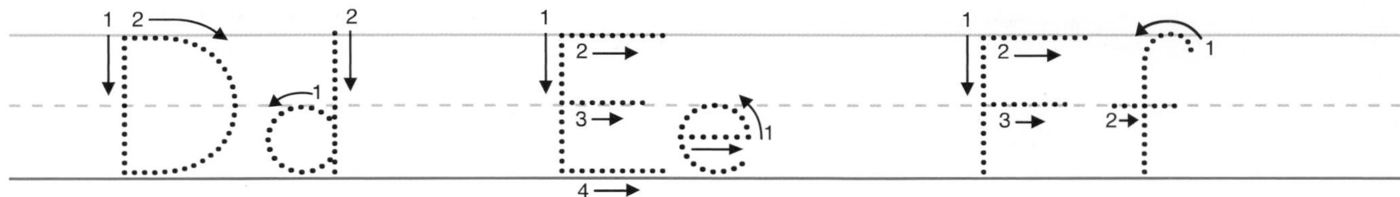

3 Listen and chant. TR: 22

4 Listen and match. TR: 23

Dd Ee Ff

LESSON

5 Video and Story

1 Watch and number. Video 2

2 Read the Unit 2 story. Circle. TR: 24

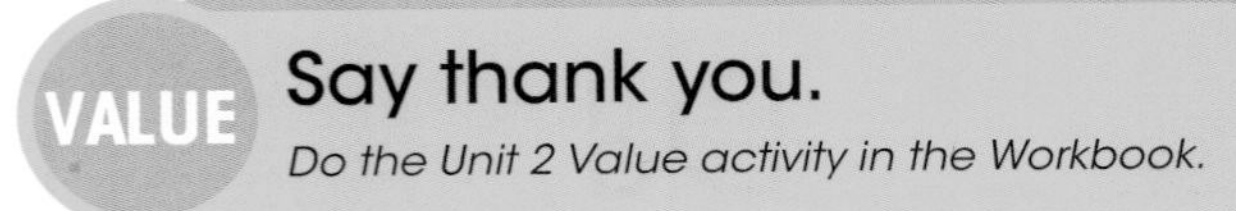

GAME 1 Look at p. 17. Cut and play.

Is it a pencil?
Yes, it is!
Two pencils!

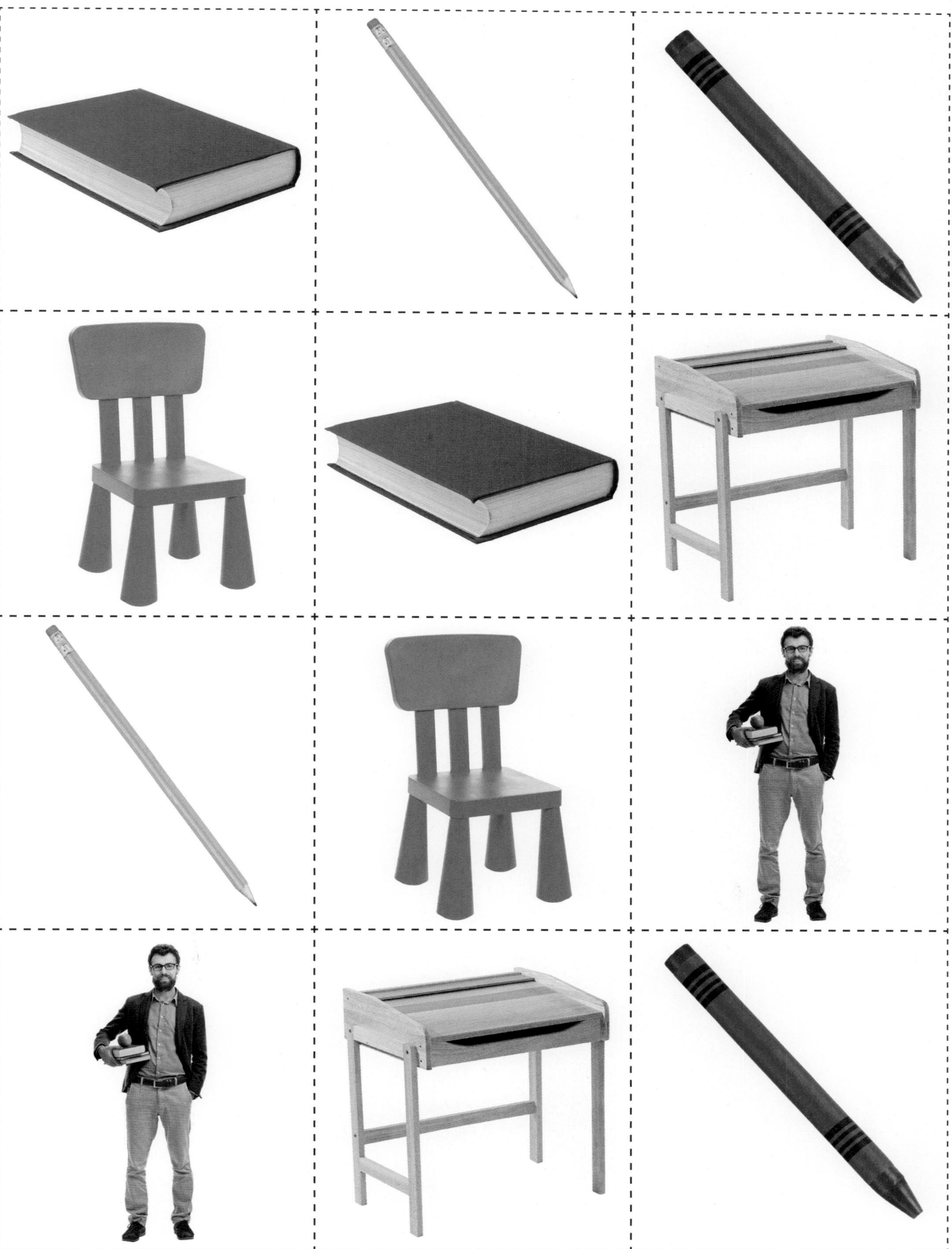

My Toys

UNIT 3

Draw your favorite toy.

LESSON

1 Words

1 Listen and point. TR: 25

ball **car** **doll** **robot** **teddy bear** **train**

2 Listen and repeat. TR: 26

3 Listen and circle. TR: 27

1.  
2. 
3. 
4.   
5.  
6.   

Grammar

What's this? It's a car.

1 Listen and repeat. TR: 28

2 Play and say.

LESSON 3

Grammar and Song

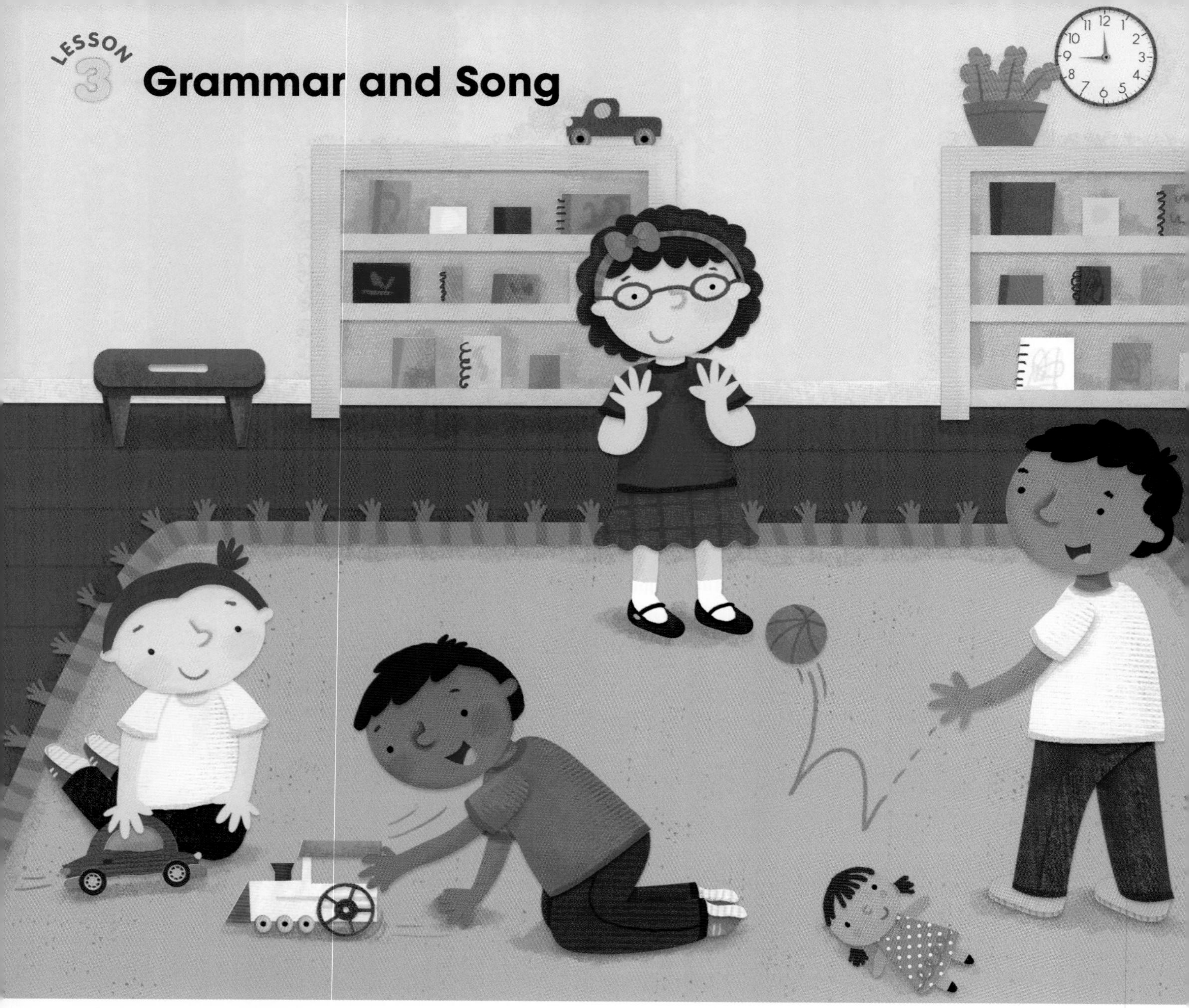

1 Listen and repeat. TR: 29

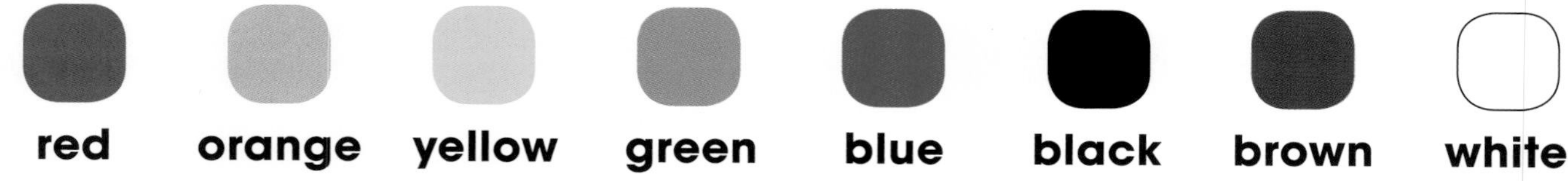

2 Listen and repeat. TR: 30

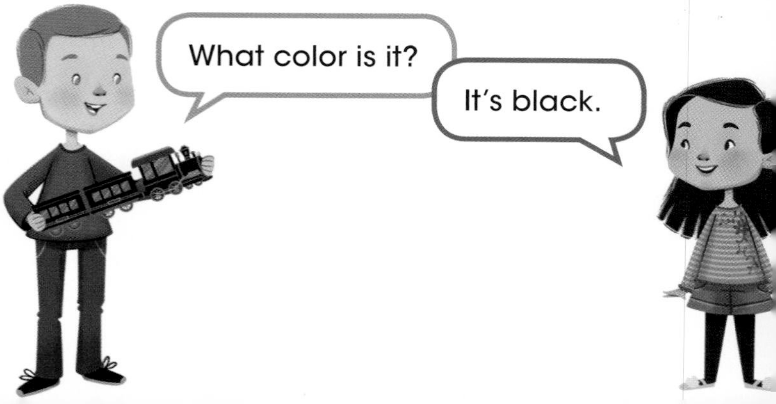

What color is it?

It's black.

3 Listen and sing. TR: 31 and 32

Phonics

1 Listen, point, and repeat. TR: 33

2 Trace the letters.

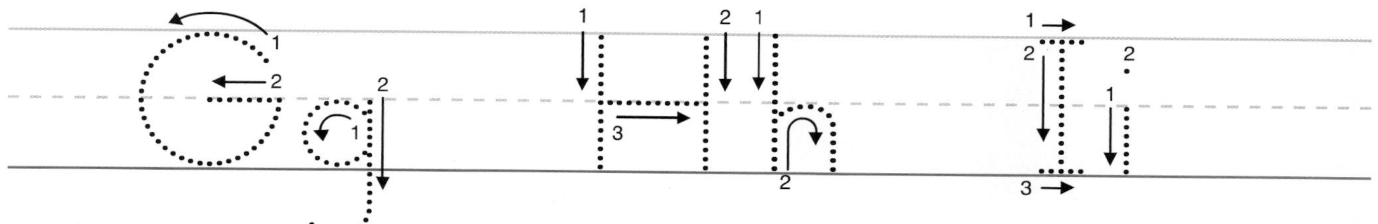

3 Listen and chant. TR: 34

4 Listen and match. TR: 35

Gg Hh Ii

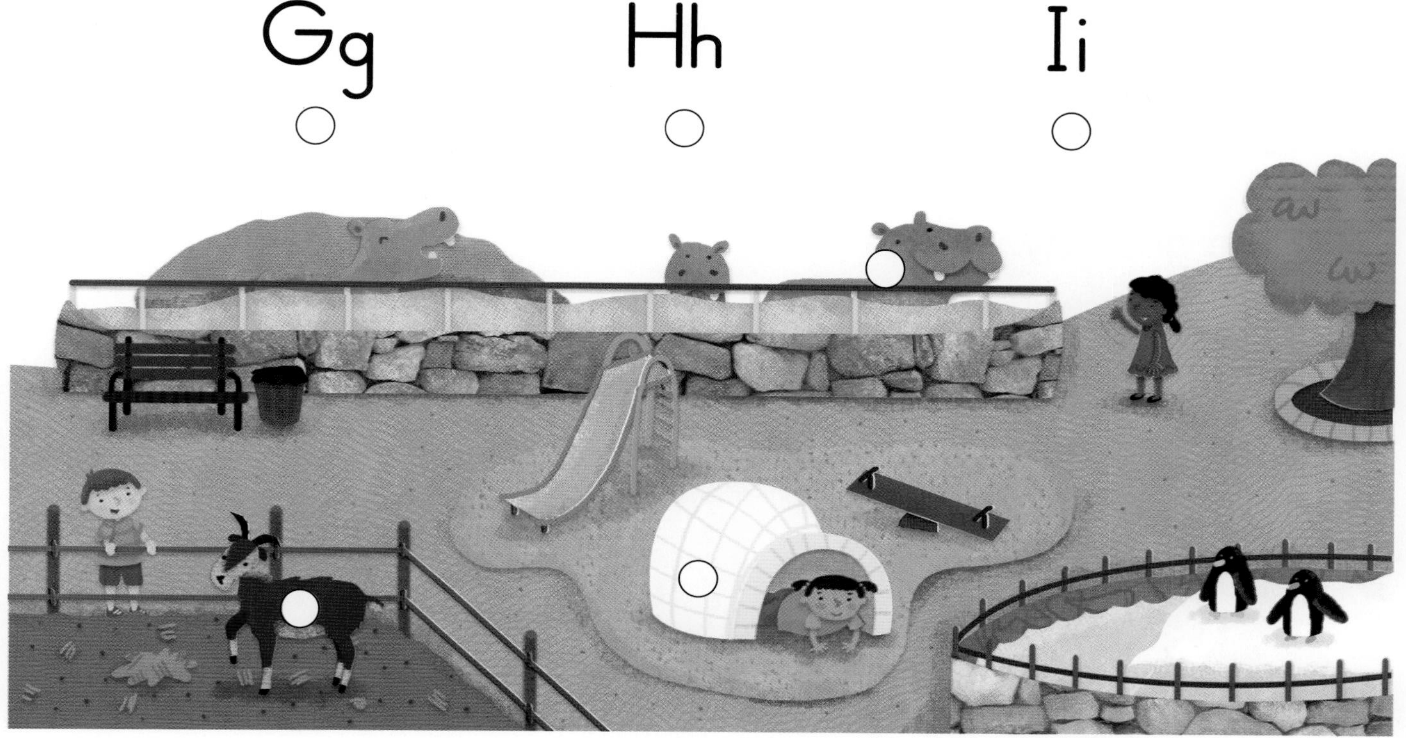

5 Video and Story

1 Watch and match. Video 3

Emilia

Juan

Kaitlyn

Mati

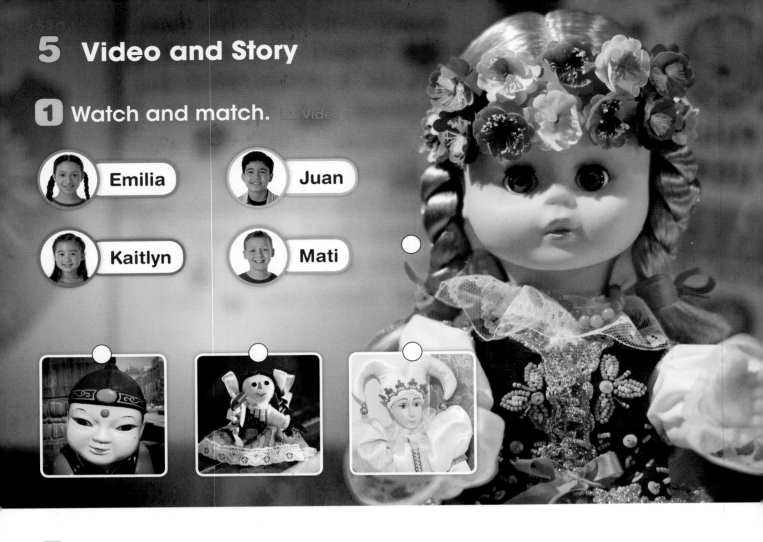

2 Read the Unit 3 story. Circle. TR: 36

VALUE Be careful.

Do the Unit 3 Value activity in the Workbook.

3 Trace and say.

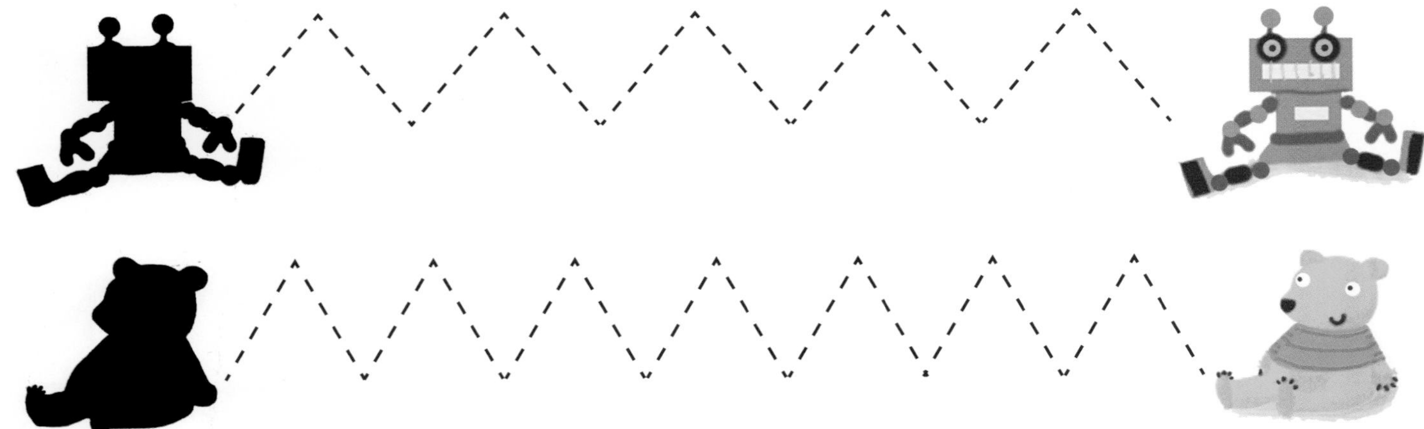

On the Farm

UNIT 4

Draw a farm.

LESSON 1
Words

1 Listen and point. TR: 37

bird

cat

cow

dog

horse

rabbit

big

small

2 Listen and repeat. TR: 38

3 Listen and number. TR: 39

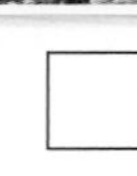

1 Listen and repeat. TR: 40

2 Play and say.

START

END

LESSON 3

Grammar and Song

1 Listen and repeat. TR: 41

1 one   2 two   3 three   4 four   5 five   6 six

7 seven   8 eight   9 nine   10 ten   11 eleven   12 twelve

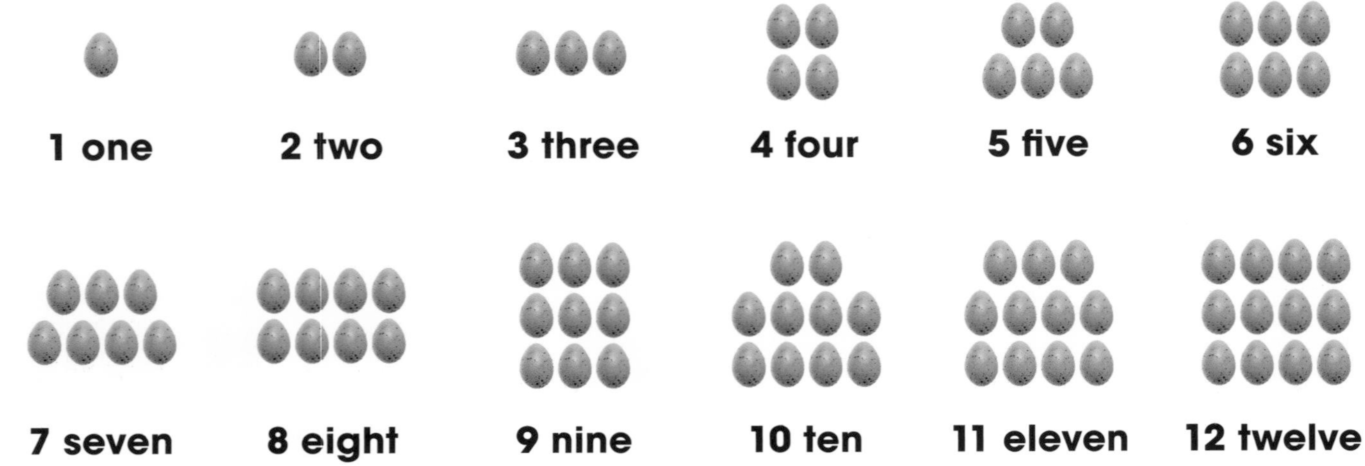

2 Listen and repeat. TR: 42

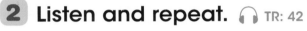

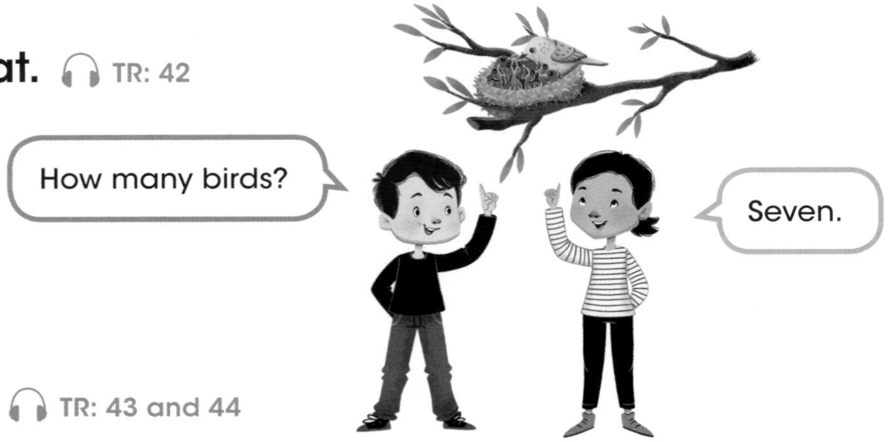

How many birds?
Seven.

3 Listen and sing. TR: 43 and 44

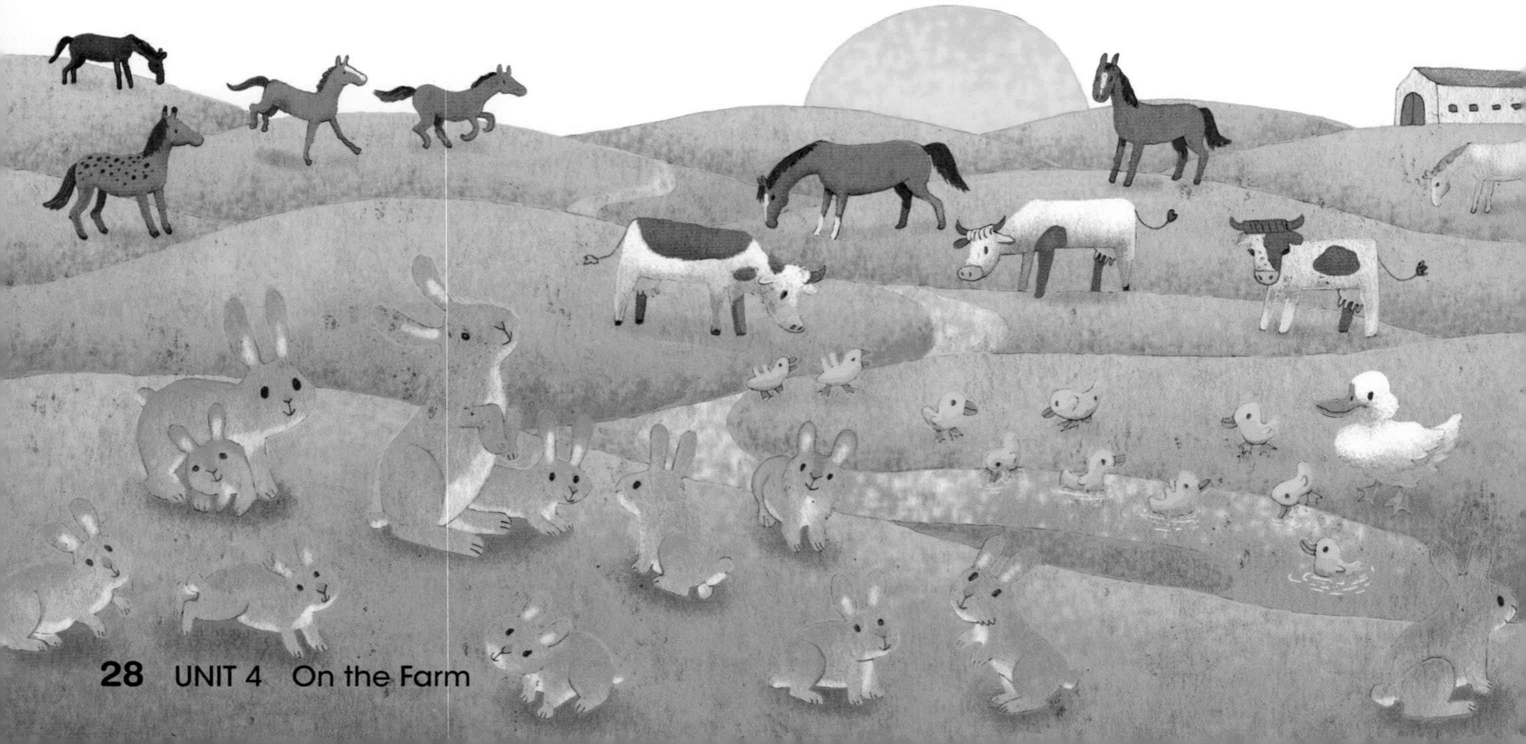

Phonics

1 Listen, point, and repeat. TR: 45

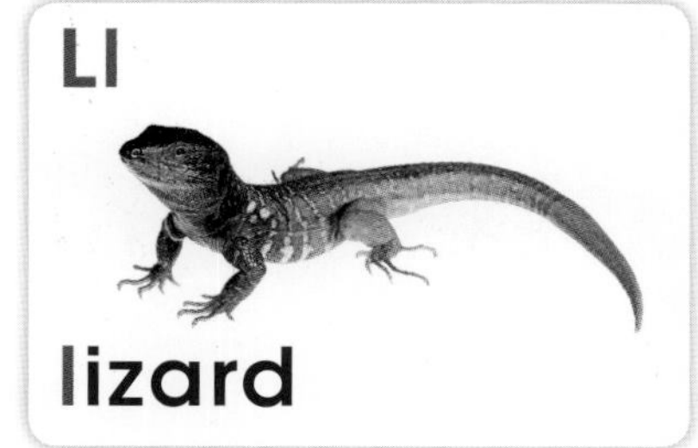

2 Trace the letters.

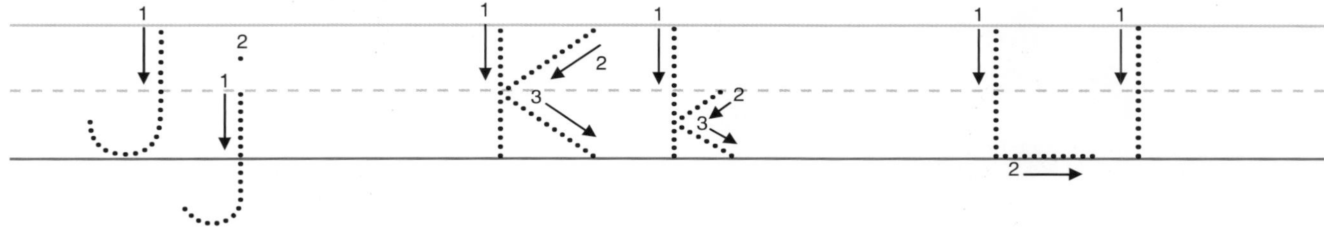

3 Listen and chant. TR: 46

4 Listen and match. TR: 47

Jj Kk Ll

LESSON 5 Video and Story

1 Watch and number. Say. Video 4

2 Read the Unit 4 story. Circle. TR: 48

VALUE **Make friends.**
Do the Unit 4 Value activity in the Workbook.

GAME 2 Look at p. 31. Cut and play.

What is it?
It's a ball.
How many balls?
One, two, three, four, five, six, seven. Seven balls.

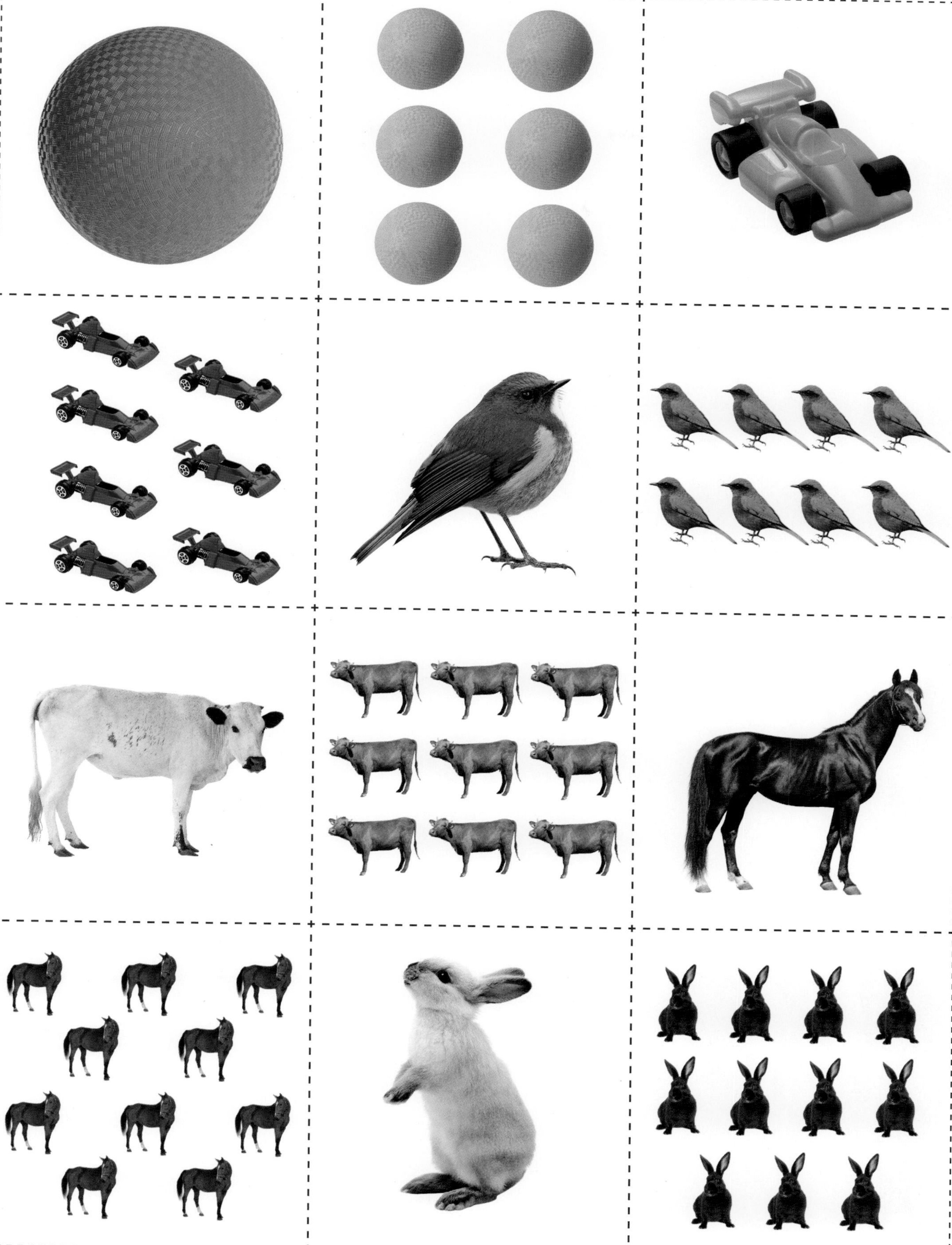

UNIT 5

I Like Food!

Draw your favorite food.

LESSON 1

Words

1 Listen and point. TR: 49

bread

chicken

fruit

juice

milk

rice

water

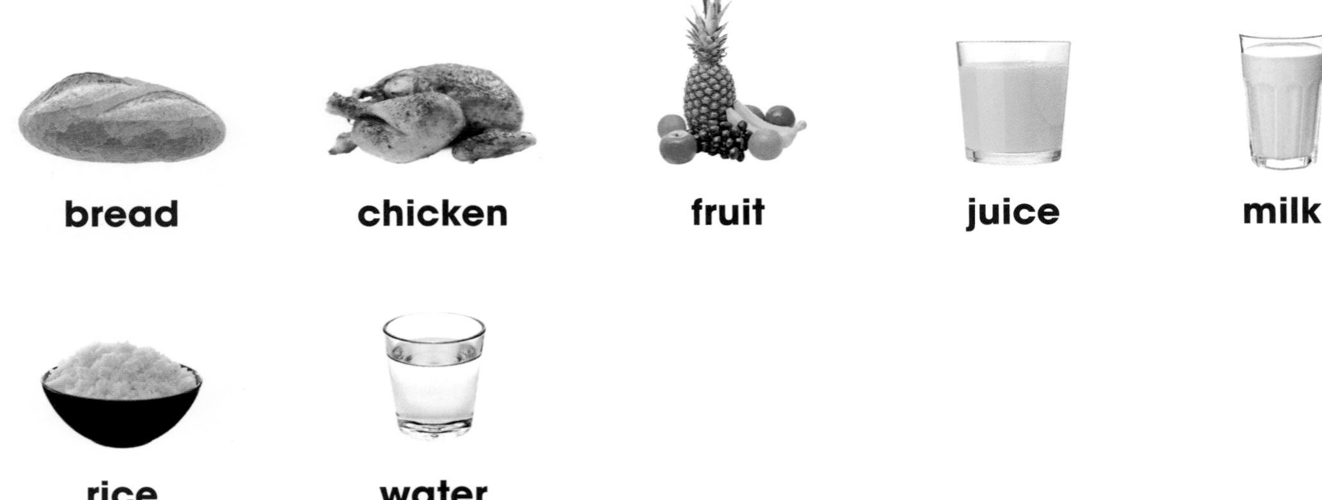

2 Listen and repeat. TR: 50

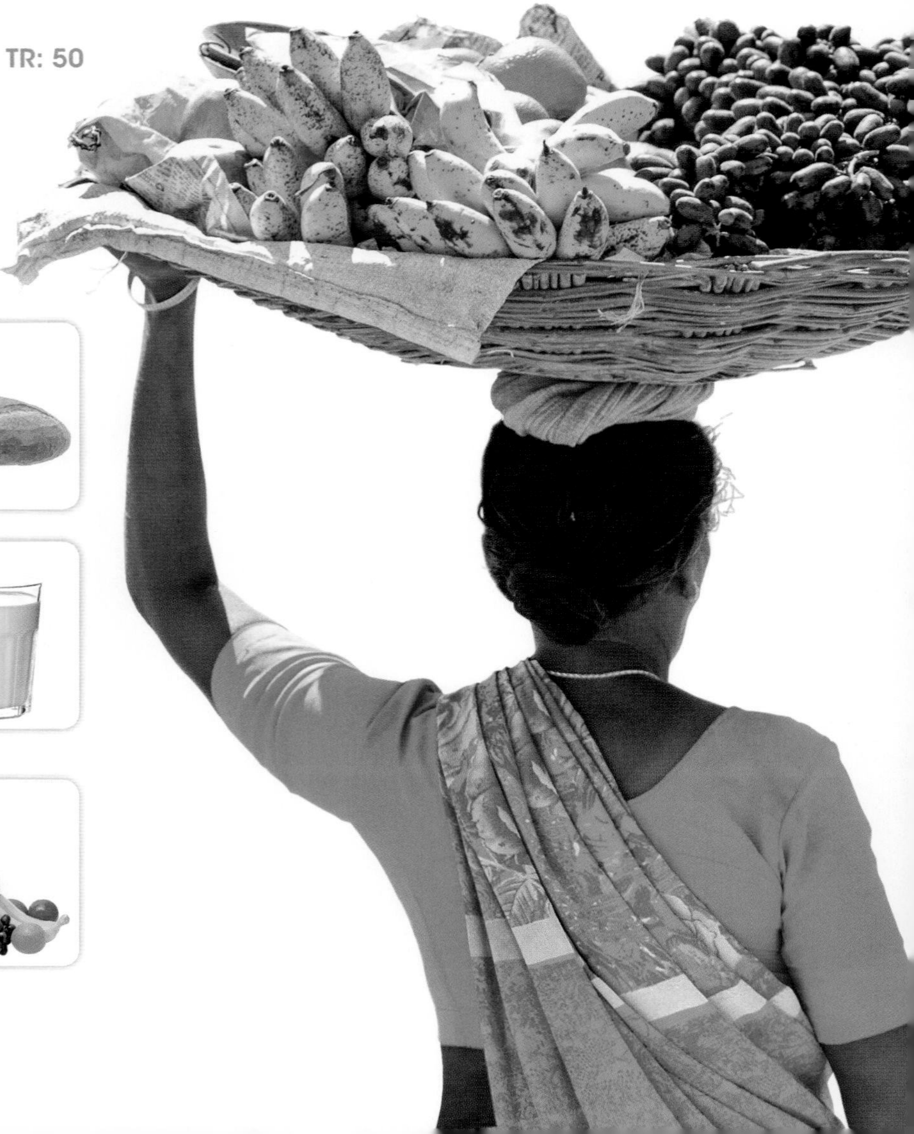

3 Listen. Write *Y* for Yes or *N* for No. TR: 51

1.

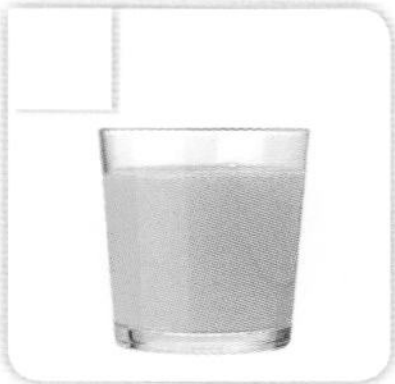

2.

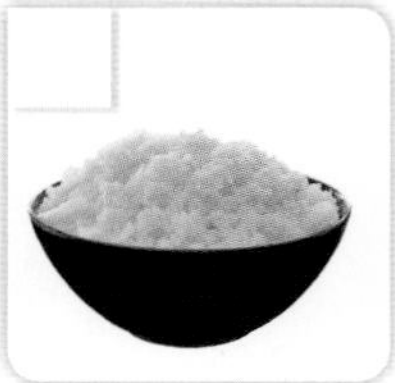

3.

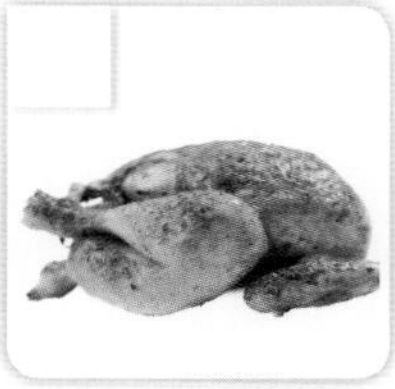

4.

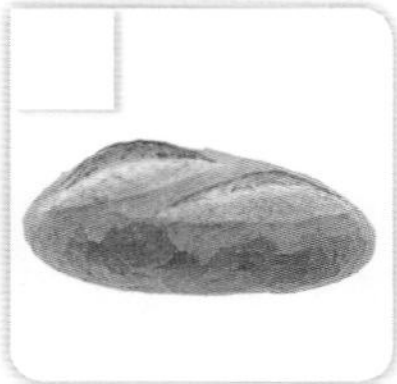

5.

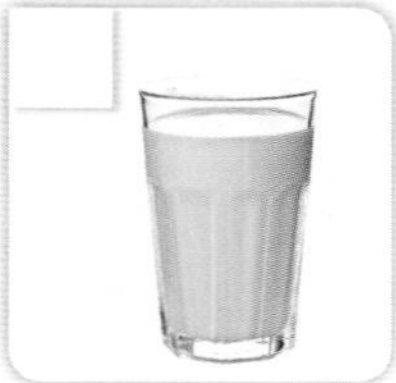

6.

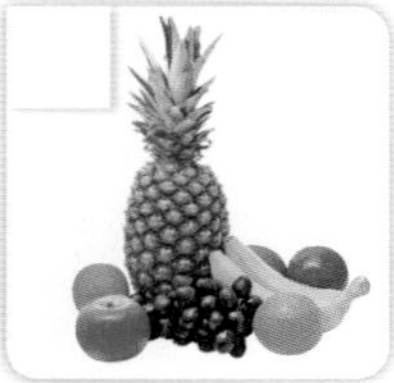

Grammar

1 Listen and repeat. TR: 52

2 Play and say.

LESSON 3 Grammar and Song

1 Listen and repeat. TR: 53

2 Listen and sing. TR: 54 and 55

Phonics

1 Listen, point, and repeat. TR: 56

2 Trace the letters.

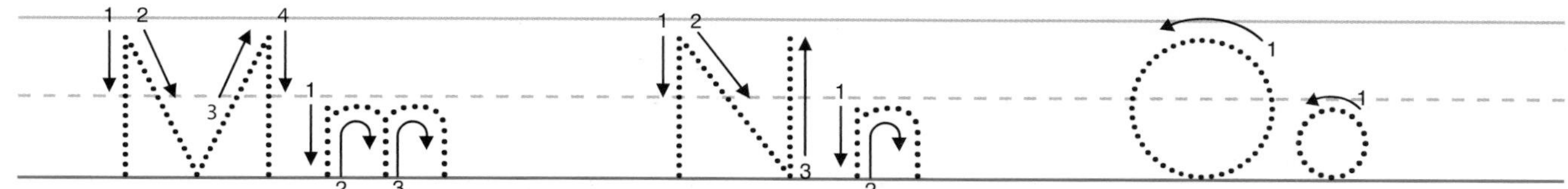

3 Listen and chant. TR: 57

4 Listen and match. TR: 58

Mm Nn Oo

LESSON 5 Video and Story

1 Watch and check (✓). Video 5

2 Read the Unit 5 story. Circle. TR: 59

VALUE Give and share.
Do the Unit 5 Value activity in the Workbook.

3 Trace and say.

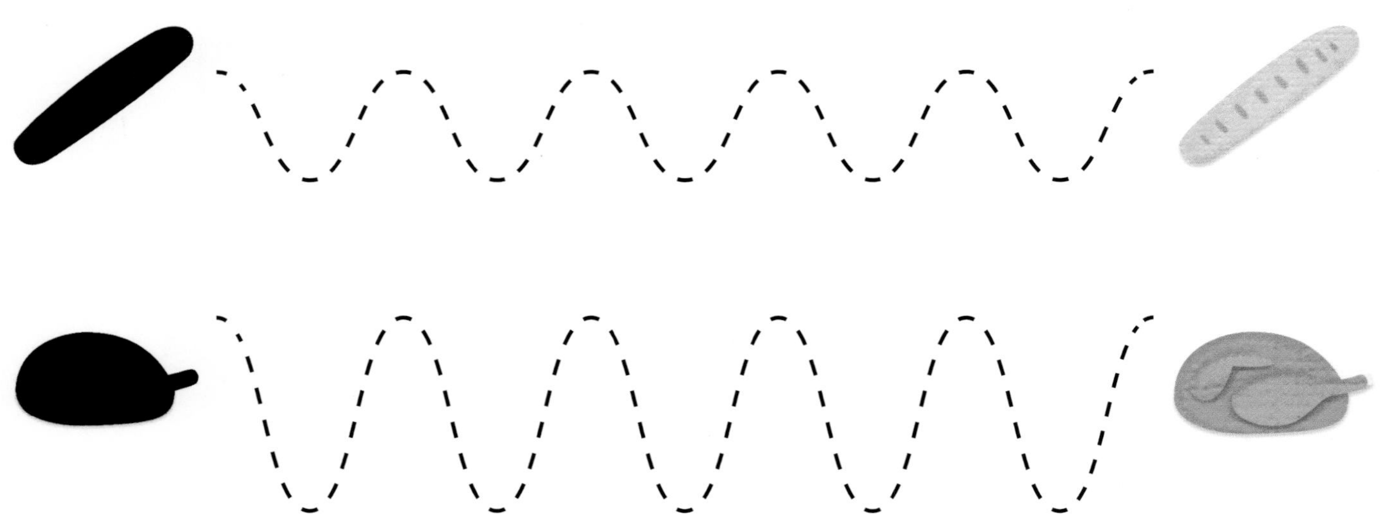

UNIT 6

How Are You?

How many boys? Count.

LESSON 1 Words

1 Listen and point. TR: 60

happy

sad

hot

cold

hungry

thirsty

2 Listen and repeat. TR: 61

3 Listen and number. TR: 62

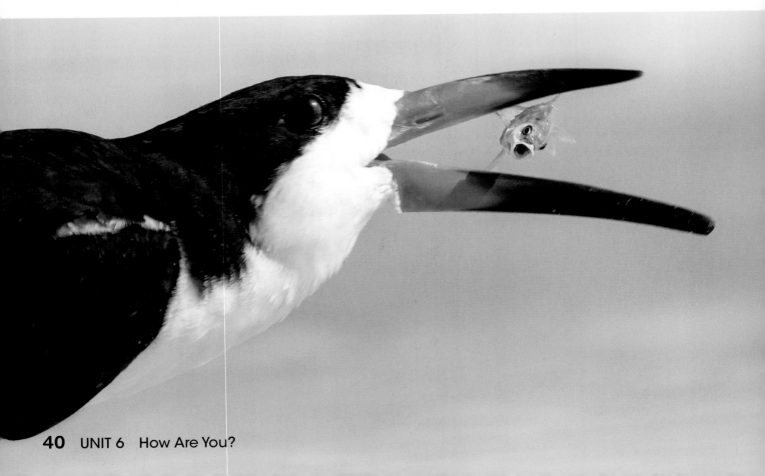

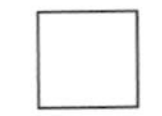

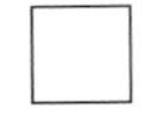

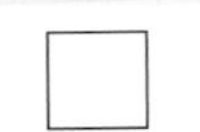

Grammar

1 Listen and repeat. TR: 63

2 Play and say.

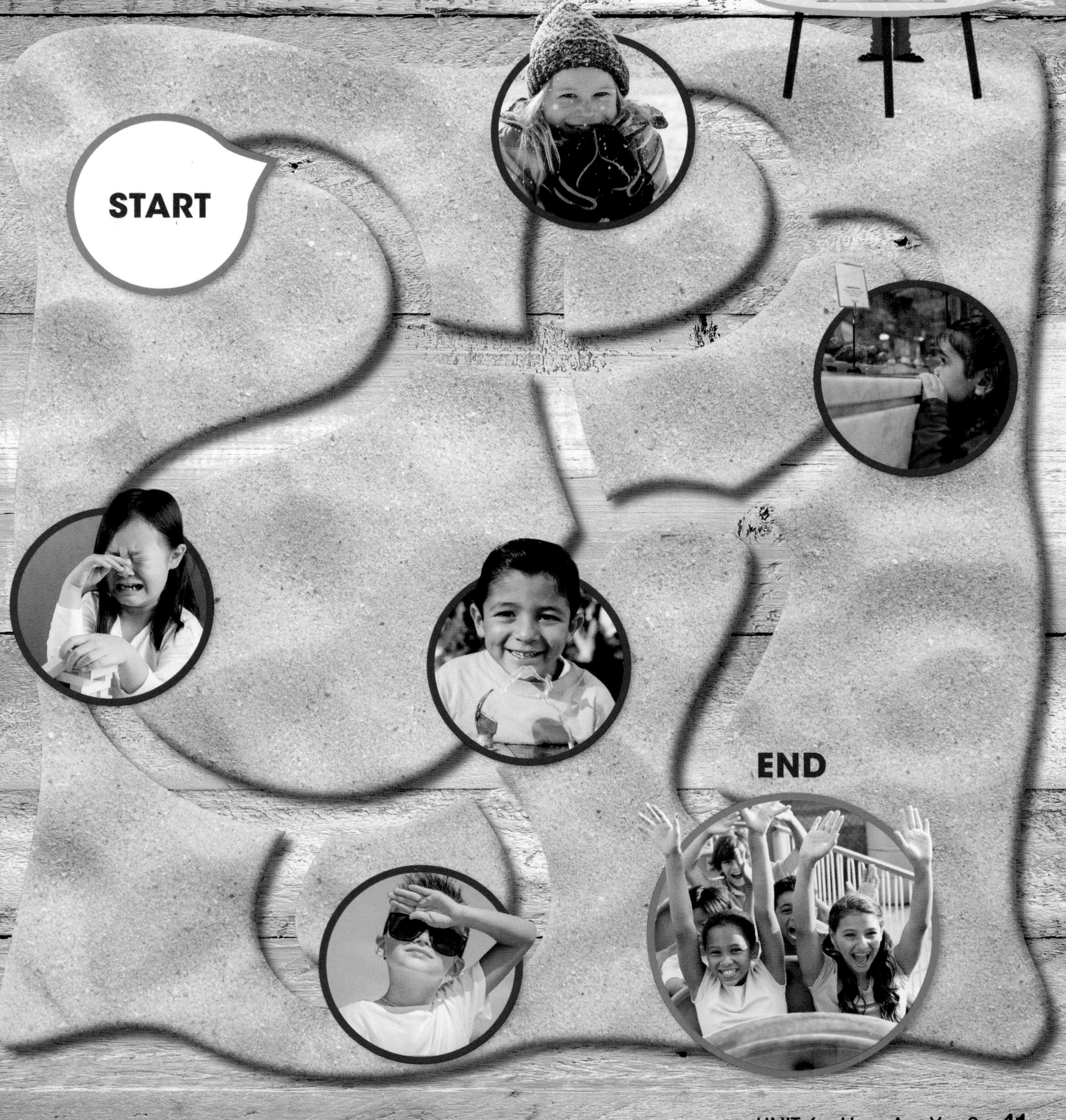

START

END

LESSON 3

Grammar and Song

1 Listen and repeat. TR: 64

2 Listen and sing. TR: 65 and 66

Phonics

1 Listen, point, and repeat. TR: 67

Pp

pink

Qq

quilt

Rr

rain

2 Trace the letters.

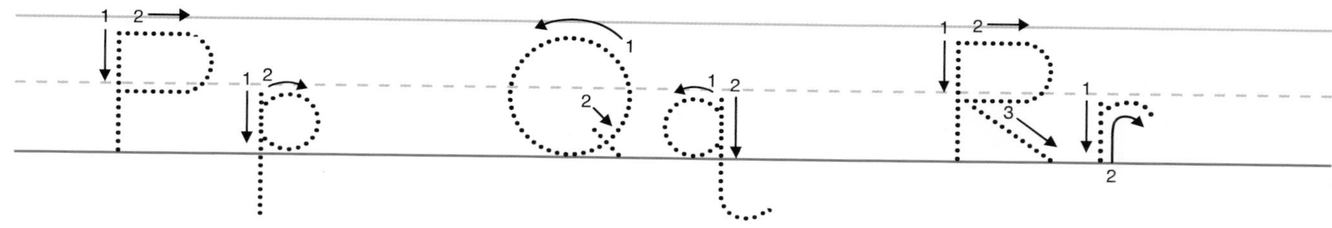

3 Listen and chant. TR: 68

4 Listen and match. TR: 69

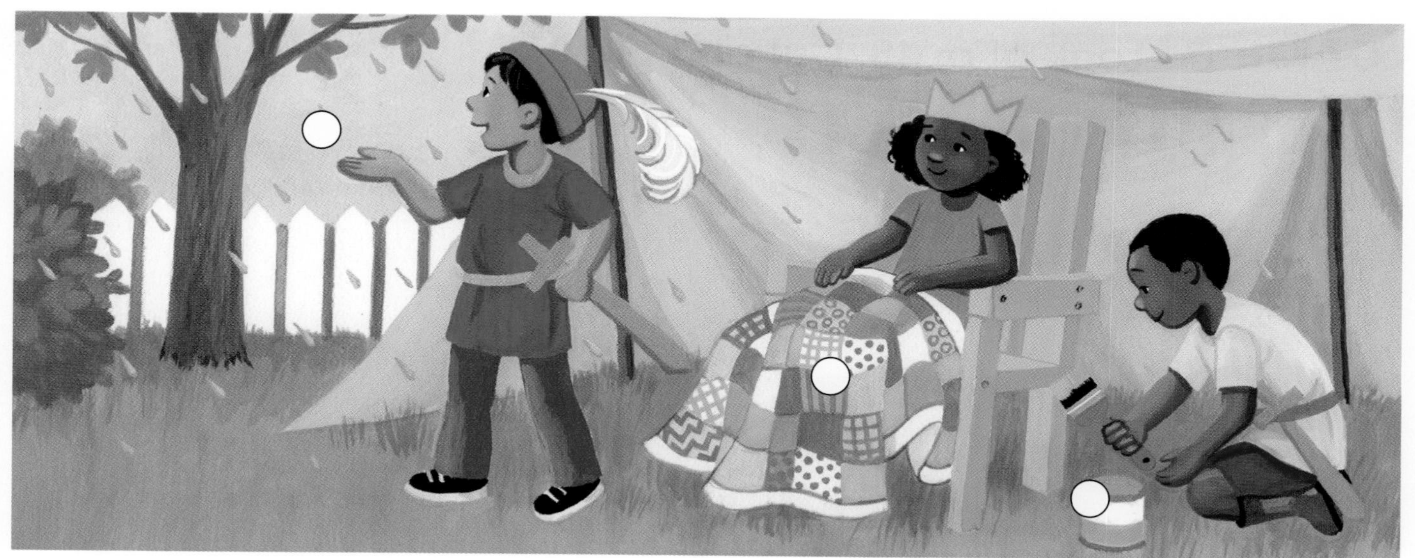

LESSON 5

Video and Story

1 Watch and match. Video 6

Aliyah

Mati

Rhiane

Shiven

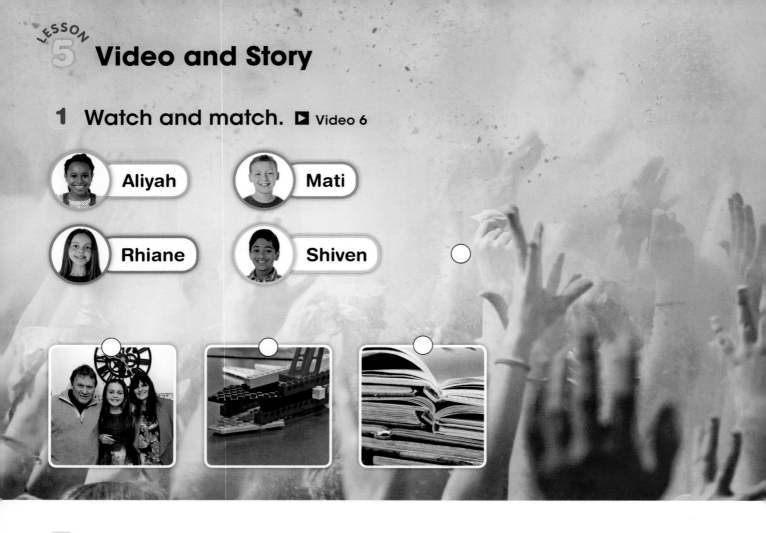

2 Read the Unit 6 story. Circle. TR: 70

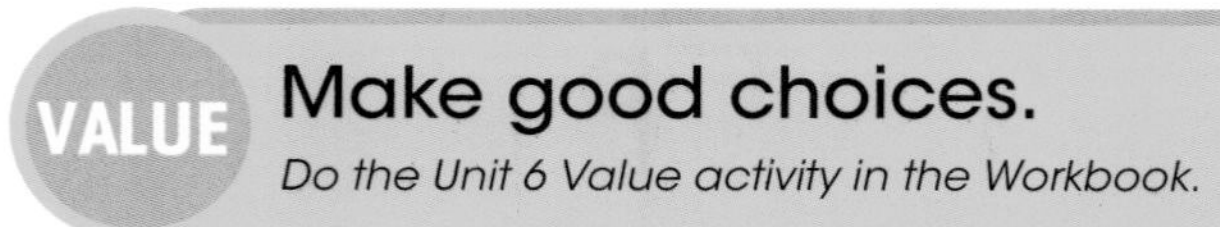

VALUE
Make good choices.
Do the Unit 6 Value activity in the Workbook.

GAME 3 Look at p. 45. Cut and play.

UNIT 7 My Family

Look. How do they feel?

LESSON 1

Words

1 Listen and point. TR: 71

mom dad sister brother grandma grandpa baby

2 Listen and repeat. TR: 72

3 Listen and number. TR: 73

Grammar

LESSON 2

1 Listen and repeat. TR: 74

2 Draw and say.

LESSON 3 Grammar and Song

1 Listen and repeat. TR: 75

2 Listen and sing. TR: 76 and 77

Phonics

1 Listen, point, and repeat. TR: 78

Ss

sun

Tt

tea

Uu

umbrella

Vv

van

2 Trace the letters.

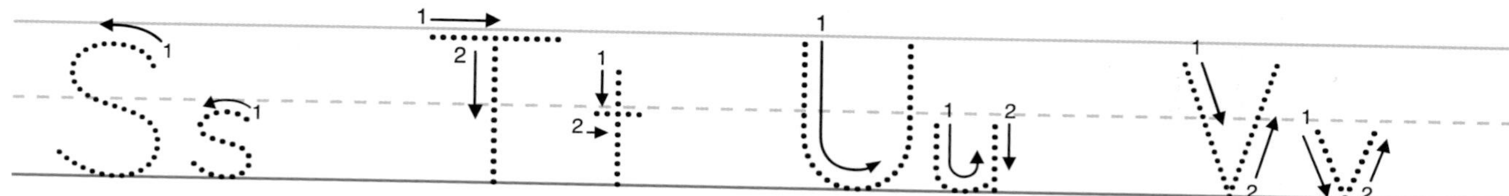

3 Listen and chant. TR: 79

4 Listen and match. TR: 80

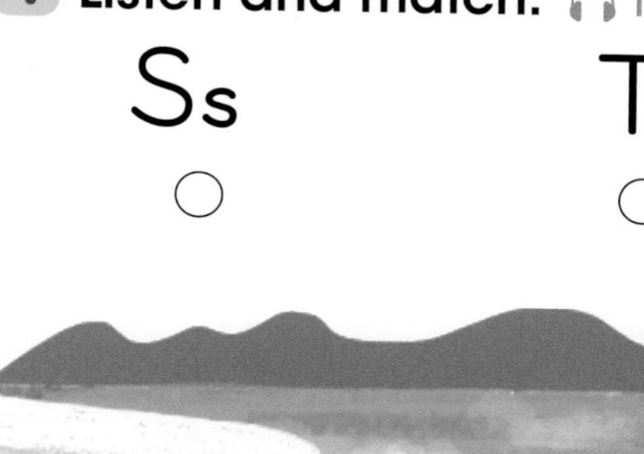

LESSON 5

Video and Story

1 Watch and match. ▶ Video 7

2 Read the Unit 7 story. Circle. TR: 81

Help others.

Do the Unit 7 Value activity in the Workbook.

3 Trace and say.

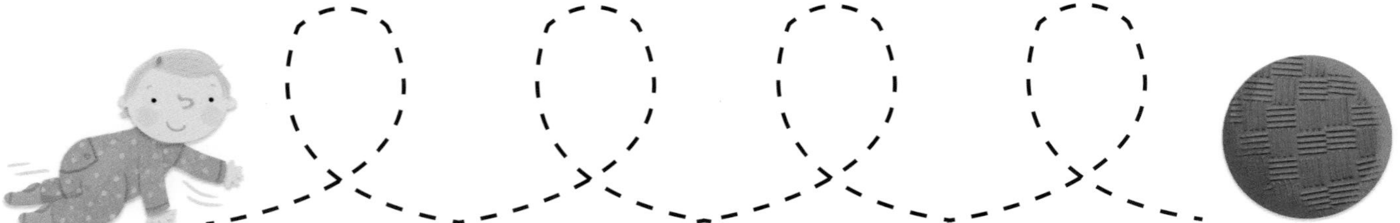

UNIT 8

My Body

Look and point. Name the colors.

LESSON 1

Words

1 Listen and point. TR: 82

2 Listen and repeat. TR: 83

3 Listen and touch. TR: 84

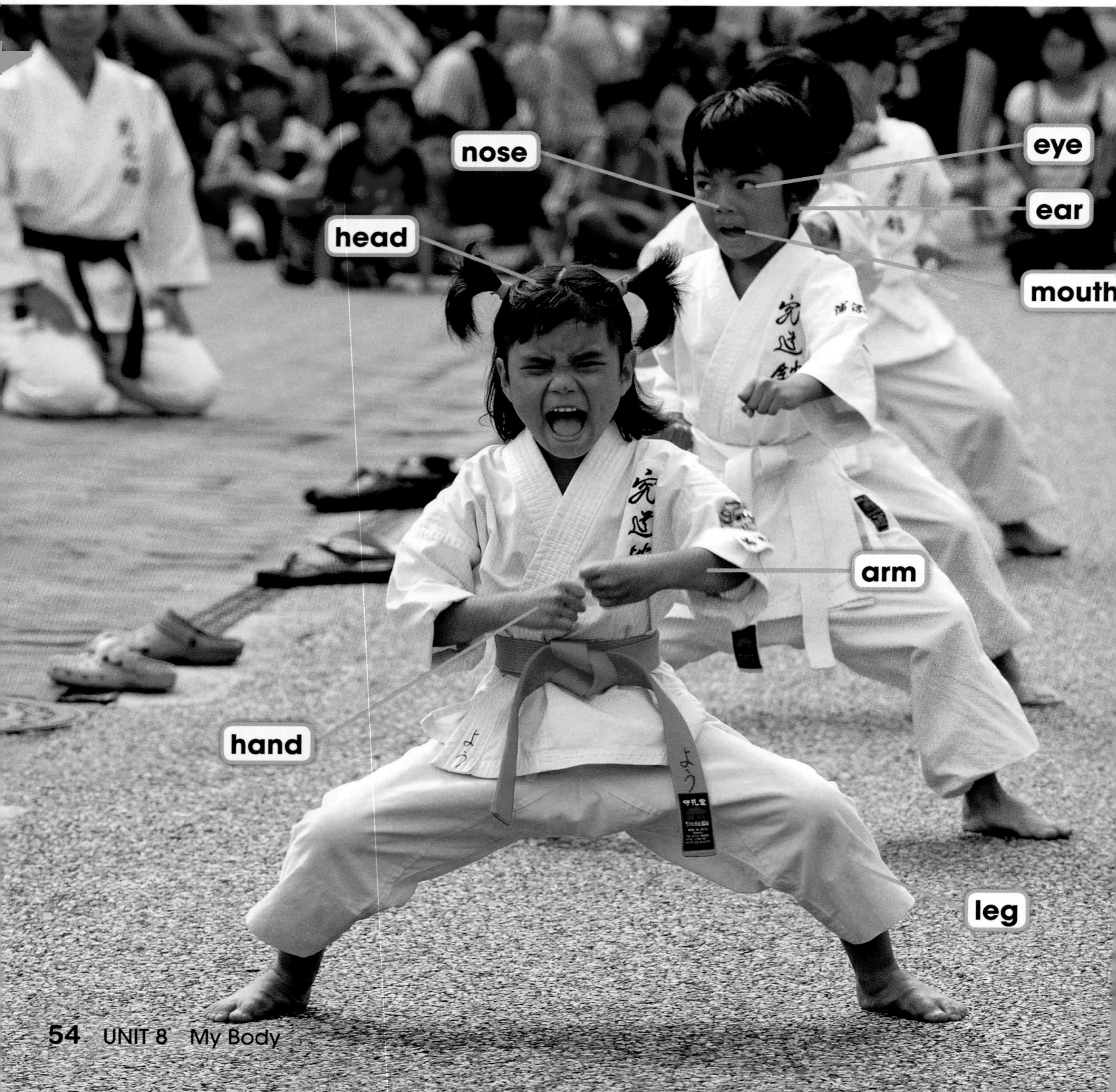

1 Listen and repeat. TR: 85

I have two hands.

2 Spin and color. Say.

LESSON 3

Grammar and Song

1 Listen and repeat. TR: 86

I have two eyes.
Are they blue?
No, they aren't.
Are they brown?
Yes, they are.

2 Listen and sing. TR: 87 and 88

Phonics

1 Listen, point, and repeat. TR: 89

Ww
water

Xx
box

Yy
yo-yo

Zz
zebra

2 Trace the letters.

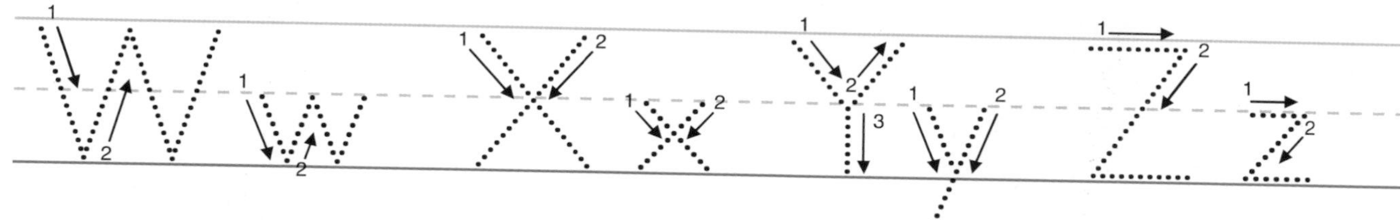

3 Listen and chant. TR: 90

4 Listen and match. TR: 91

Zz

LESSON 5

Video and Story

1 Watch and match. Video 8

Rhiane

Yurara

2 Read the Unit 8 story. Circle. TR: 92

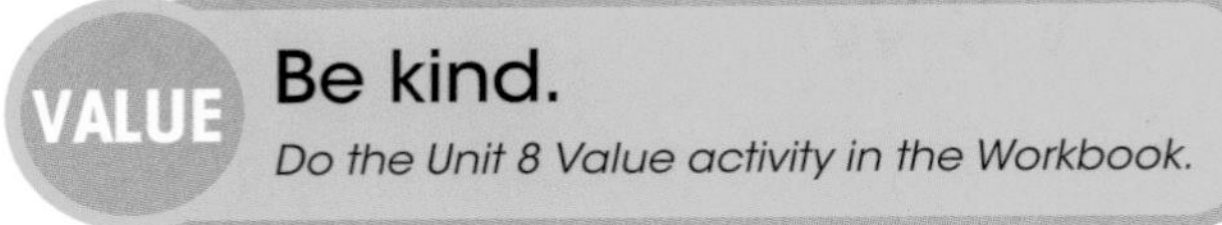

VALUE
Be kind.
Do the Unit 8 Value activity in the Workbook.

GAME 4 Look at p. 59. Cut and play.

I have one hand!

UNIT 9 My Clothes

Look. What can you see?

LESSON 1
Words

1 Listen and point. TR: 93

dress hat shirt shoes shorts skirt socks pants

2 Listen and repeat. TR: 94

3 Listen and circle. TR: 95

Grammar

1 Listen and repeat. TR: 96

2 Play and say.

Here is my shirt.
Here are my socks.
Here are my shorts!
SCHOOL

LESSON 3

Grammar and Song

1 Listen and repeat. TR: 97

2 Listen and sing. TR: 98 and 99

My hat is blue.

Your shirt is orange.

Phonics

1 Listen, point, and repeat. TR: 100

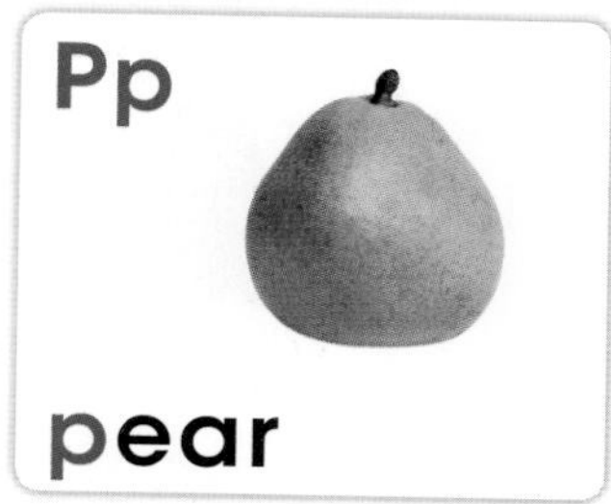

2 Listen and chant. TR: 101

3 Listen and match. TR: 102

Bb

Pp

4 Listen and circle. TR: 103

1. 

B P

2. 

B P

3. 

B P

4. 

B P

Marcel Safia Shiven

Tracy Jessica

2 Read the Unit 9 story. Circle. TR: 104

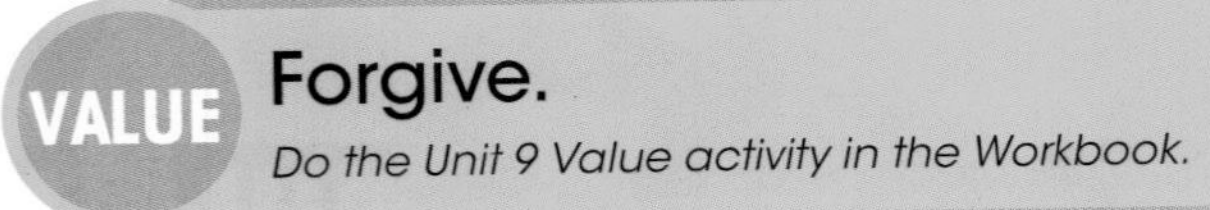

VALUE
Forgive.
Do the Unit 9 Value activity in the Workbook.

3 Trace, color, and say.

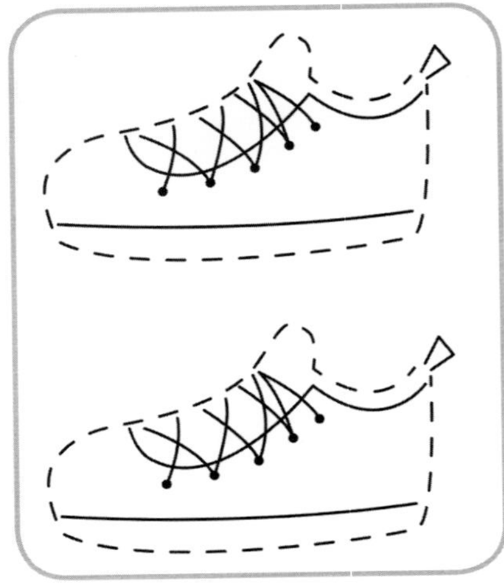

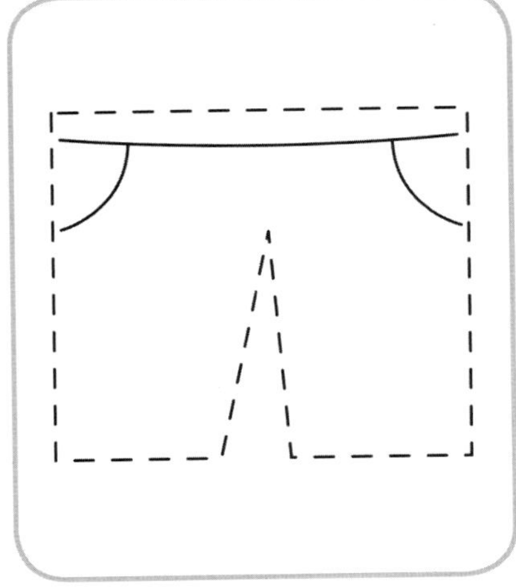

Let's Play!

UNIT 10

Look at the photo.
What can you see?

LESSON 1

Words

1 Listen and point. TR: 105

climb

draw

jump

kick

paint

play

run

swim

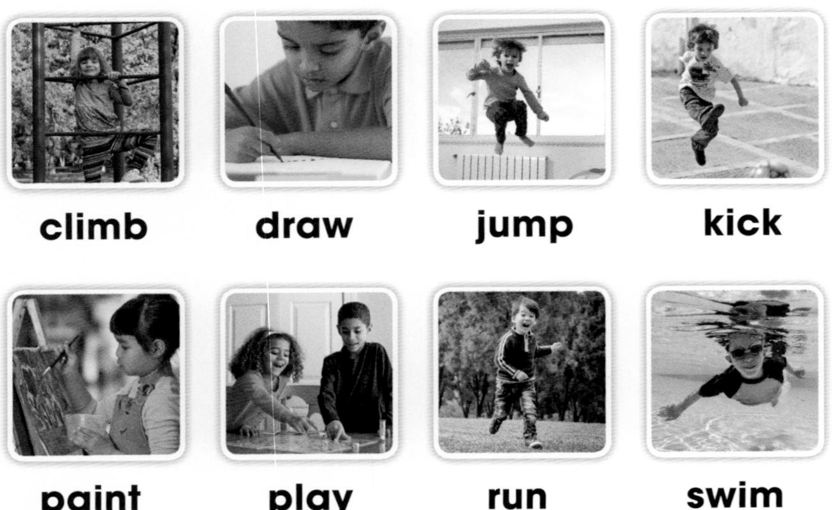

2 Listen and repeat. TR: 106

3 Listen and number. TR: 107

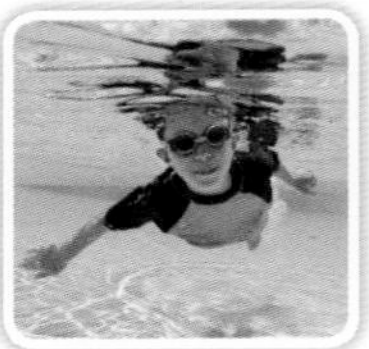

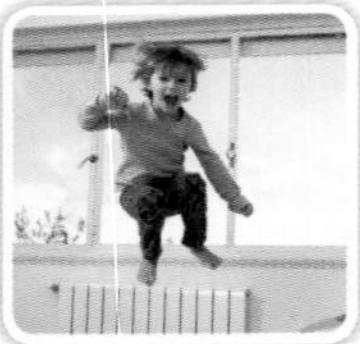

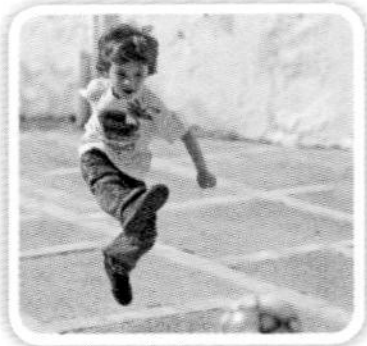

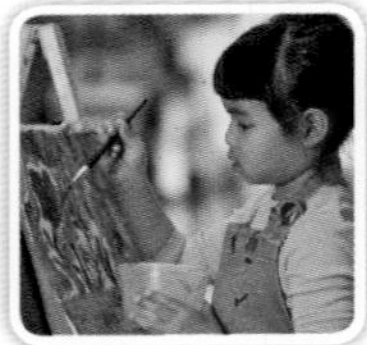

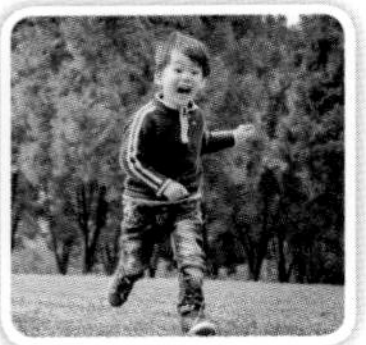

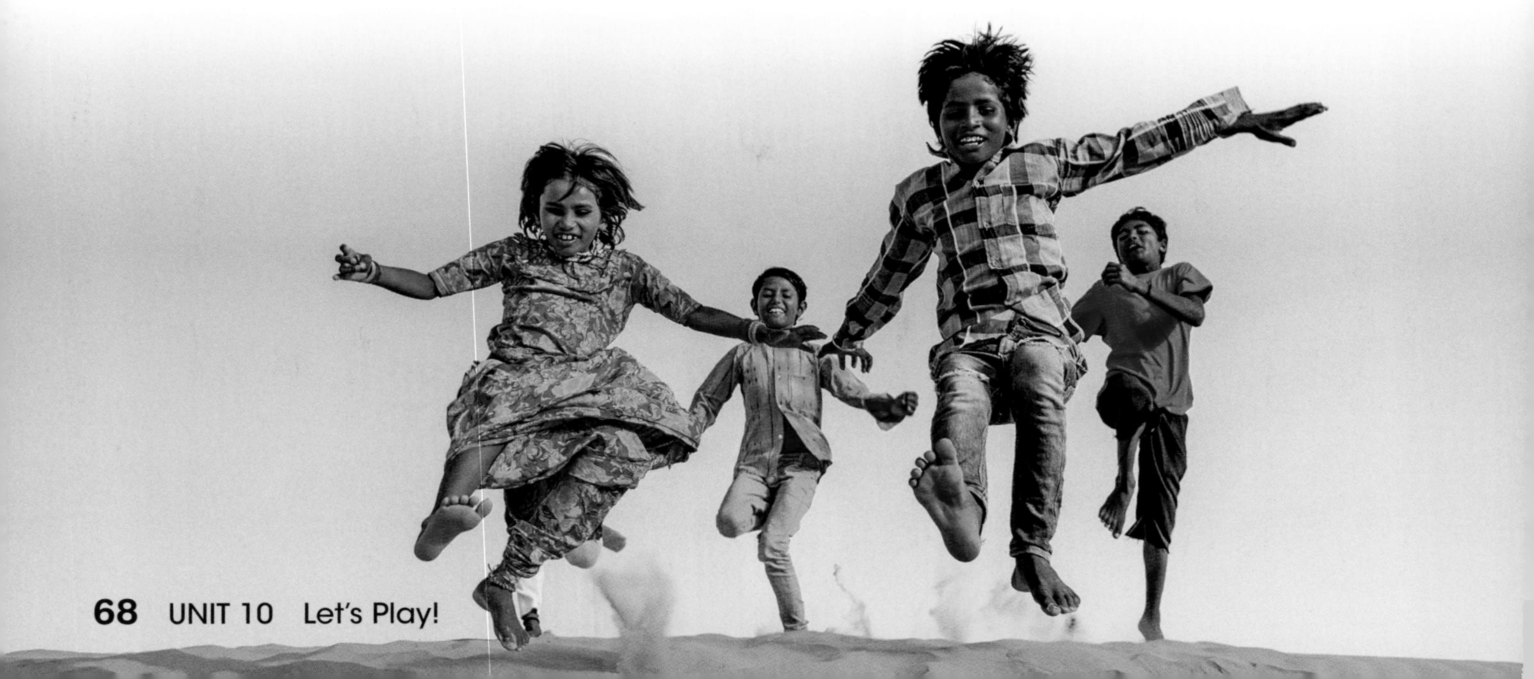

1 Listen and repeat. TR: 108

I can run.

2 Play and say.

LESSON 3

Grammar and Song

1 Listen and repeat. TR: 109

1 2 3 4 5 6 7 8 9 10 11 12

13 thirteen

14 fourteen

15 fifteen

16 sixteen

17 seventeen

18 eighteen

19 nineteen

20 twenty

2 Listen and repeat. TR: 110

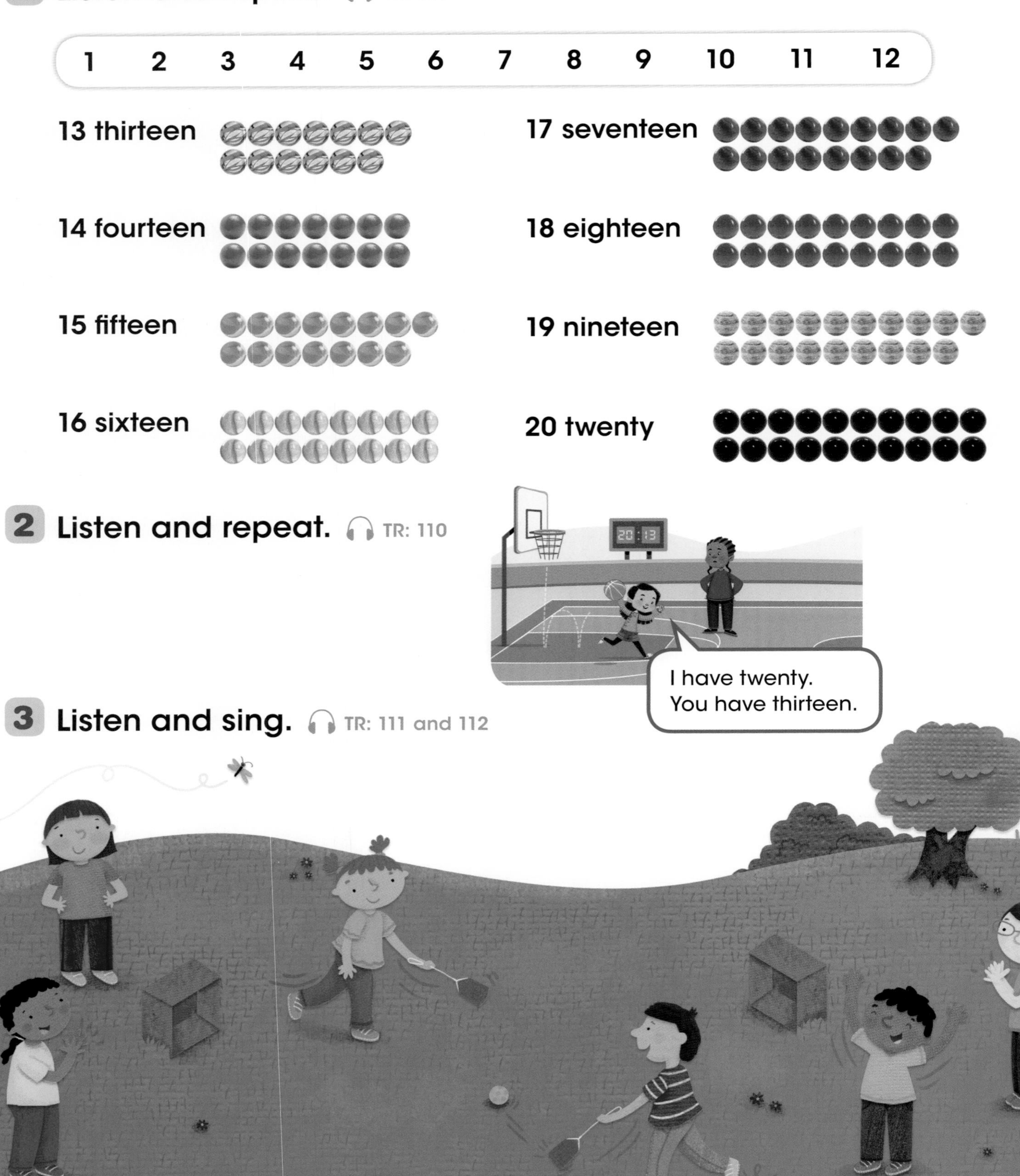

3 Listen and sing. TR: 111 and 112

1 Listen, point, and repeat. TR: 113

Dd

down

Tt

town

2 Listen and chant. TR: 114

3 Listen and match. TR: 115

Dd ○ Tt ○

4 Listen and circle. TR: 116

1. D T
2. D T
3. D T
4. D T

LESSON 5

Video and Story

1 Watch and match. Video 10

Aliyah

Kaitlyn

Marcel

Rafi

2 Read the Unit 10 story. Circle. TR: 117

VALUE **Be kind to animals.**
Do the Unit 10 Value activity in the Workbook.

GAME 5 Look at p. 73. Cut, listen, and play. TR: 118

13	14	15	16
17	18	19	20

Goodbye!

VALUE Be friendly.

✔ We read the story.

____

Fold

Unit 1

What's Your Name?

Hello, Dan.

Hello, Kim.

Hello. My name's Dan.
My name's Kim.
What's your name?
Hello. My name's Tom.
How are you?
I'm fine, thank you.

Fold

Crayons!
One, two, three, four, five, six.
Six crayons! Thank you!

4

VALUE Say thank you.

✔ We read the story. ____________

Fold

Unit 2

The Present

Is it a pencil?

No, it isn't.

1

Is it a bag?

No, it isn't.

Fold

Is it a book?

No, it isn't!

4

VALUE Be careful.

✔ We read the story.

Fold

Unit 3

Toy Box

What's this?

It's a car.

Yes! It's blue.

1

What's this?

It's a train.

Yes. It's red.

Fold

What's this?

It's a doll.

Yes. What
color is it?

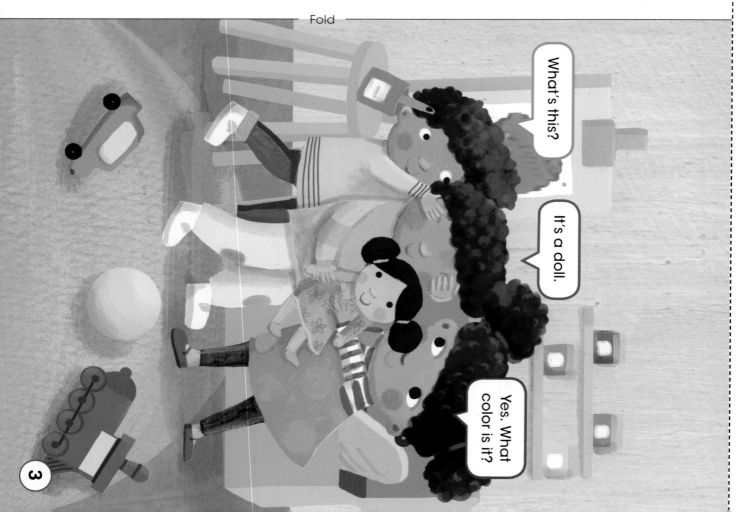

Nine, ten, eleven...

Twelve! Twelve rabbits!

VALUE Make friends.

✔ We read the story. ________

Fold

Unit 4

How Many Rabbits?

Dad, what are they?

They're rabbits.

How many rabbits?

Two.

Fold

How many rabbits?

Three, four, five...

Six, seven, eight...

Here you are!

Thank you!

4

VALUE Give and share.

✔ We read the story. ____________

Fold

Unit 5

Let's Eat!

What's this?

It's juice. I like juice.

I don't like juice.

1

What's this?

It's bread. I like bread.

I don't like bread.

Fold

What's this?

It's cake. I like cake.

I like cake, too!

I'm hungry, too! Cake?
No, thanks. I want fruit!
Fruit? OK. I like fruit.
I want an apple.

4

VALUE Make good choices.

✔ We read the story. ______

Fold

Unit 6

Snack Time

Hi, Marco.
Hi, Emi. How are you?
I'm thirsty!

1

Juice?

No, thank you.
I want water.

Fold

Hi, Marco.

Hi, Fede.
How are you?

I'm hungry!

VALUE Help others.

✔ We read the story. ______

Fold

Unit 7

The Helper

This is my dad. He's hot. Here, Dad!

Thank you!

Fold

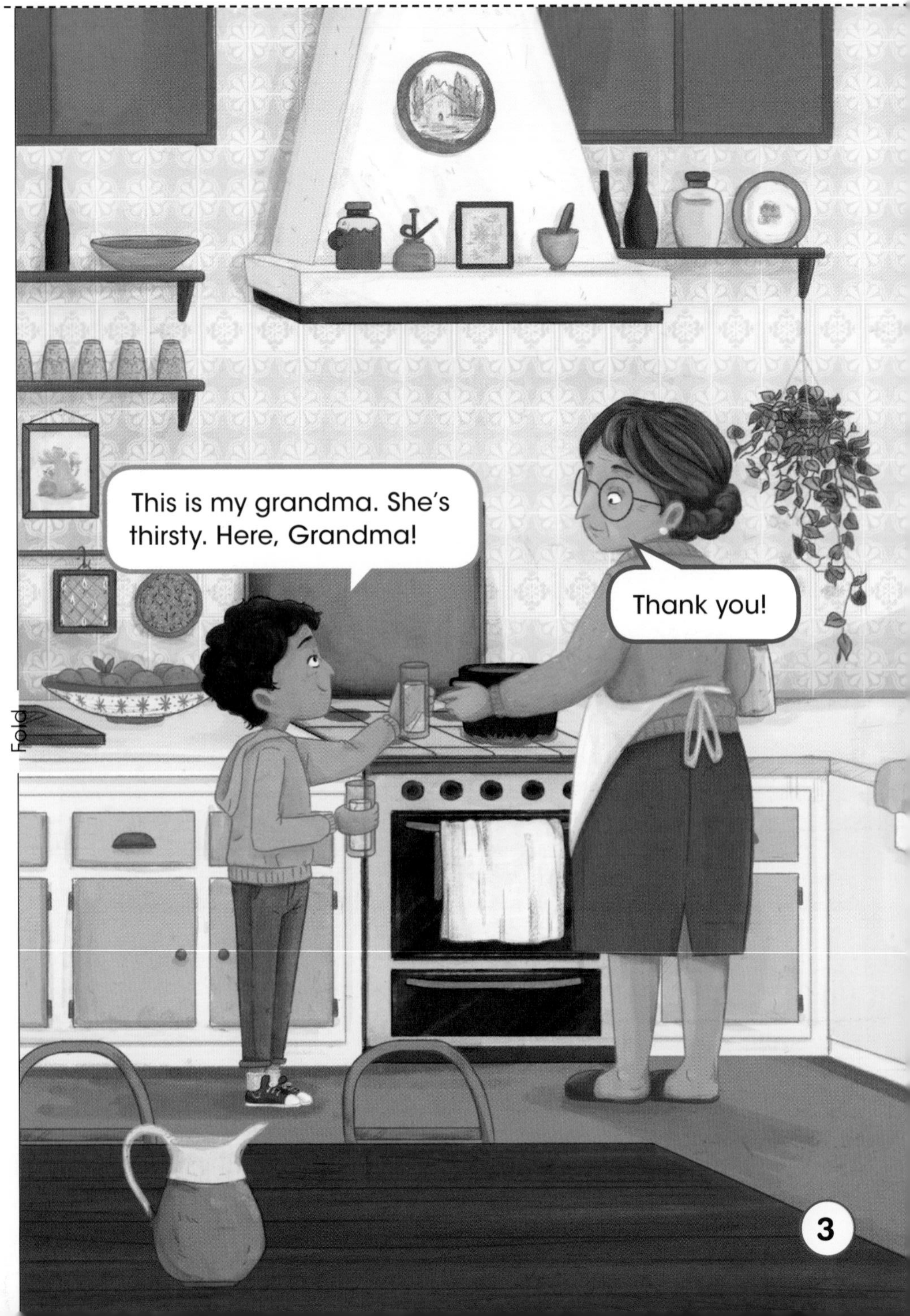

This is my grandma. She's thirsty. Here, Grandma!

Thank you!

Look at me!

Wow! A big eye,
a blue nose,
a small mouth...
I like your mask!

VALUE Be kind.

✔ We read the story.

Fold

Unit 8

The Masks

Look at me!
I have six eyes!
Yes! They're
blue and green.

Fold

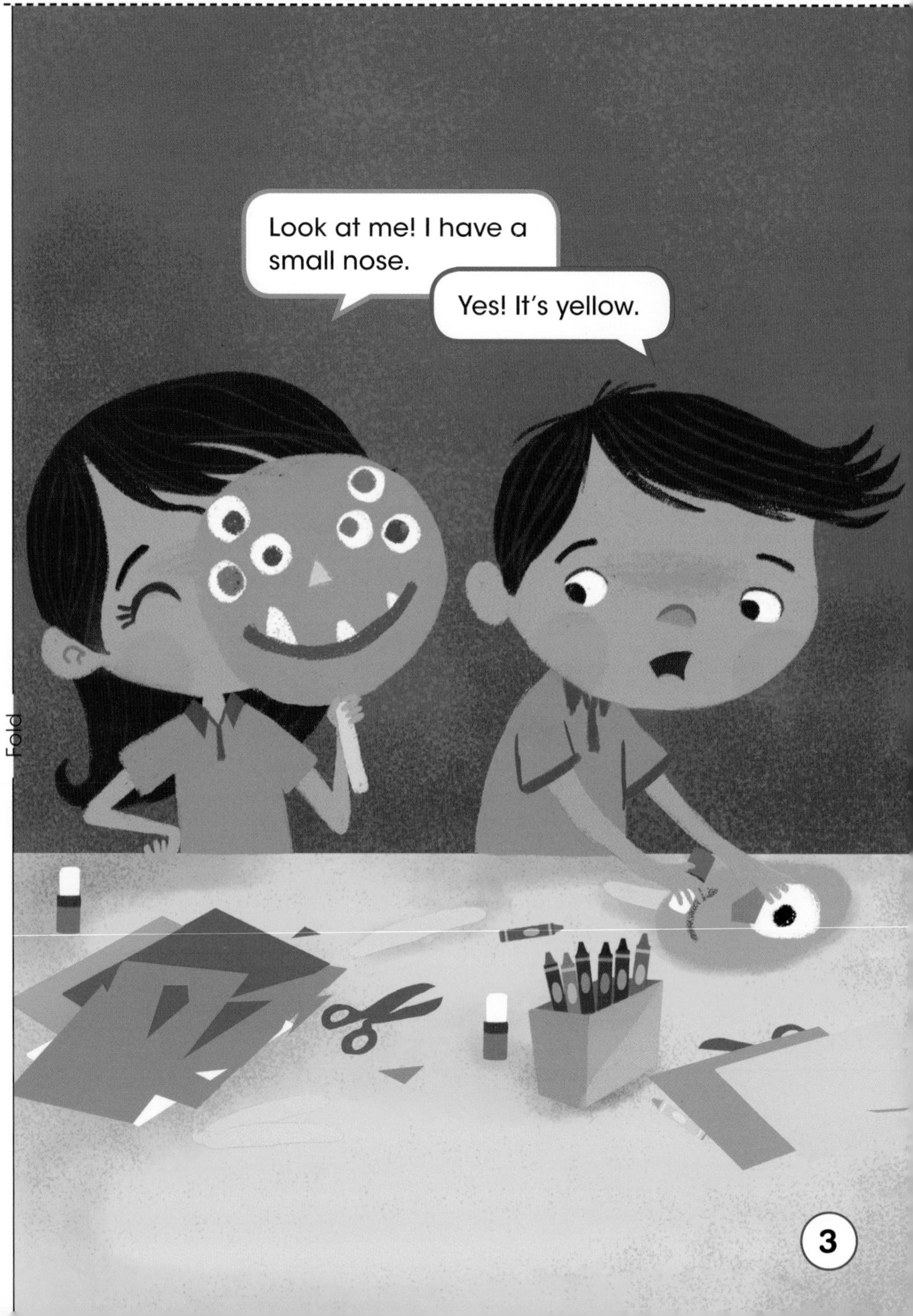

Look at me! I have a small nose.

Yes! It's yellow.

VALUE Forgive.

✔ We read the story. ______

Unit 9

The Sock

Here is my shirt.

Is it white?

No, it isn't. It's pink.

Fold

Fold

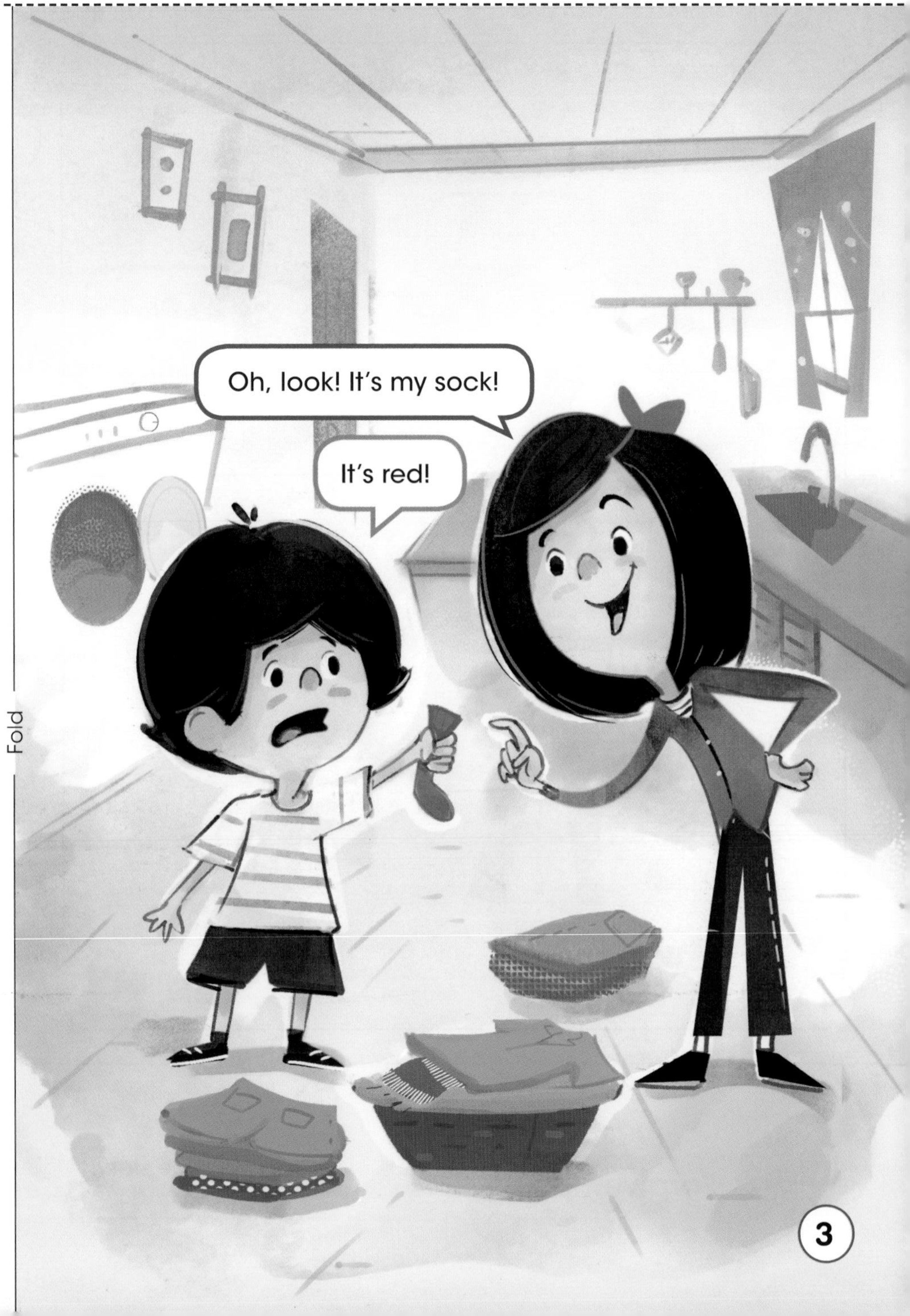

Oh, look! It's my sock!

It's red!

Let's play with the dog!
OK!

VALUE Be kind to animals.

✔ We read the story. ____________

Fold

Unit 10

Can We Play?

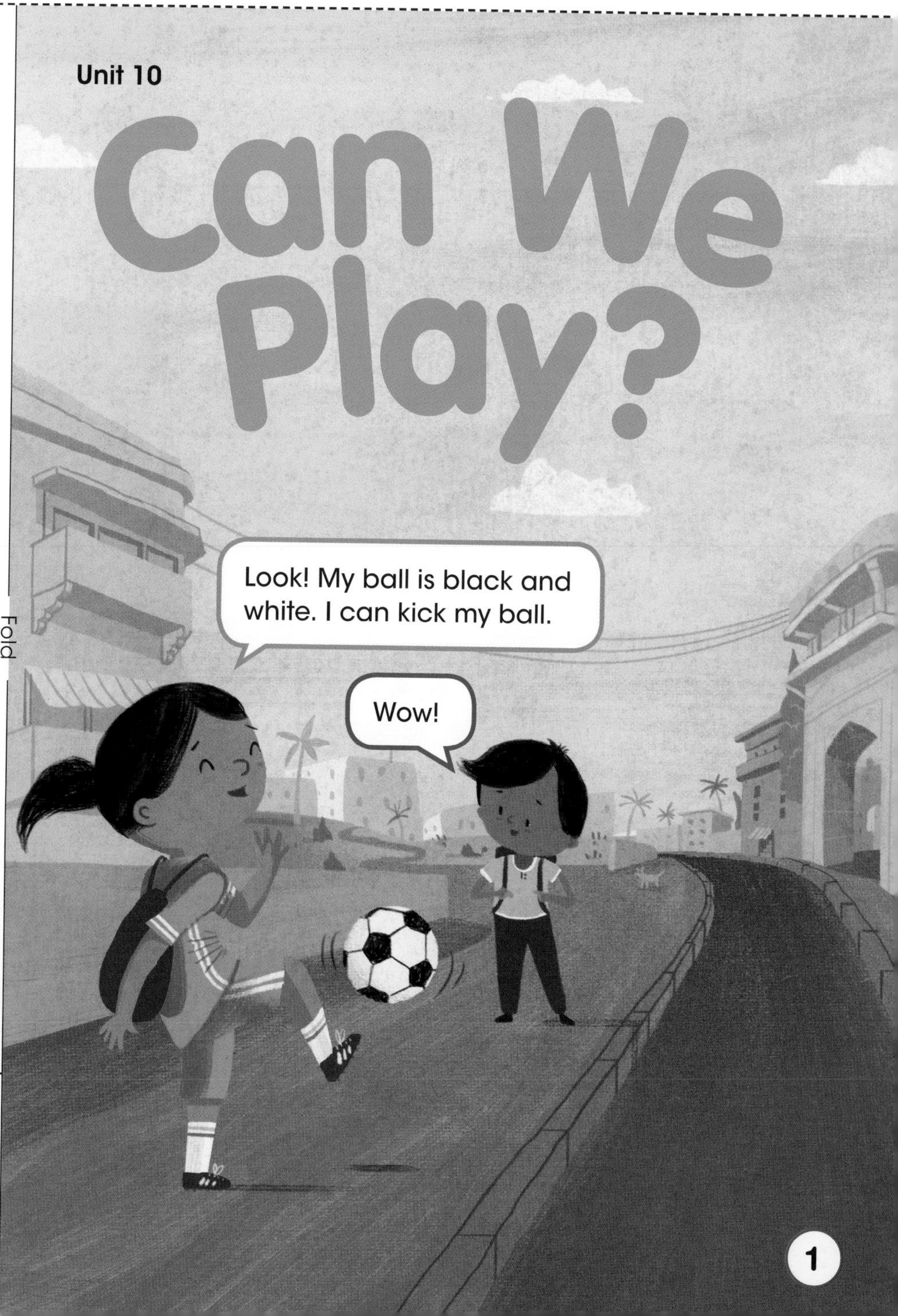

Look! My ball is black and white. I can kick my ball.

Wow!

Fold

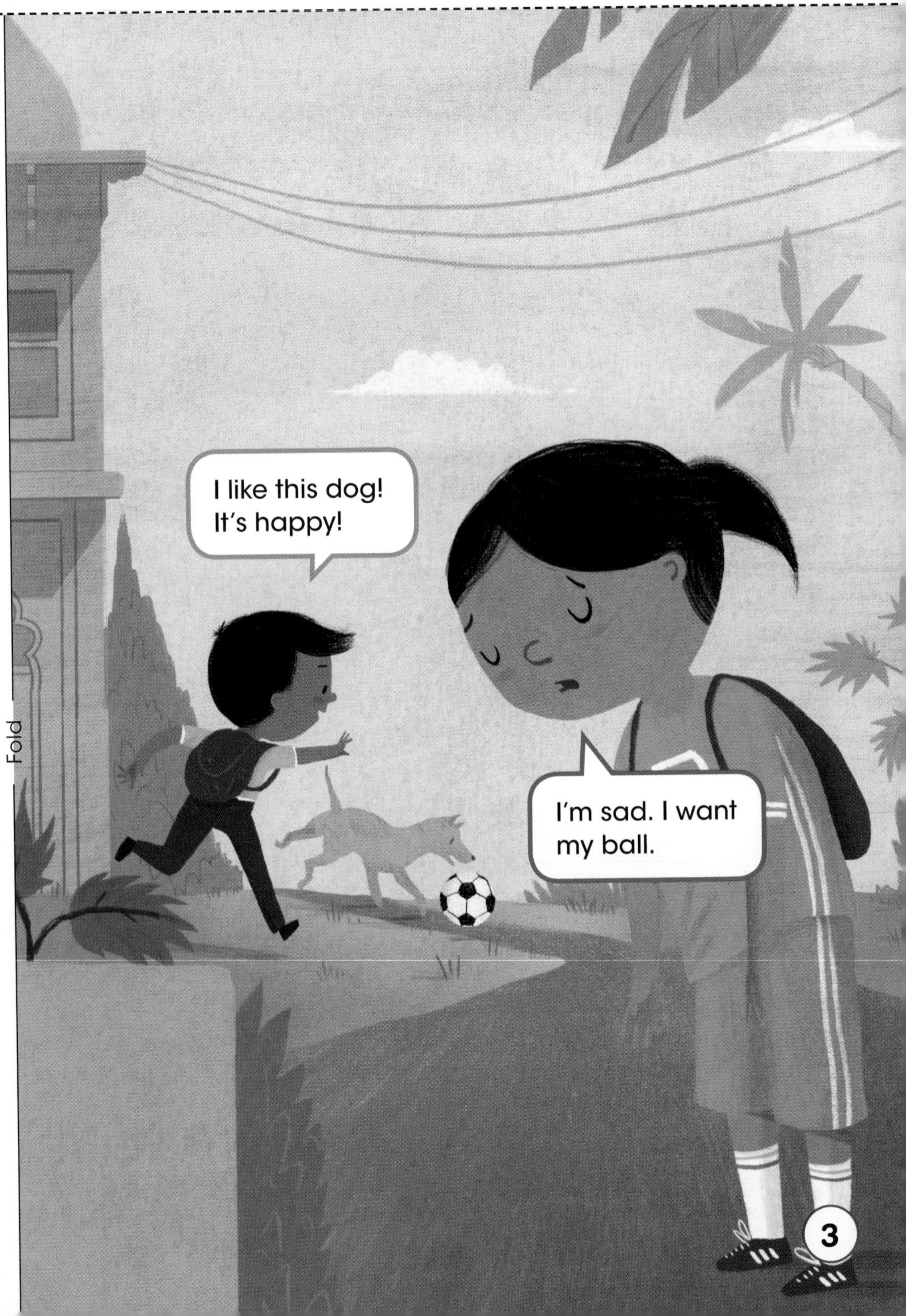

I like this dog!
It's happy!

I'm sad. I want
my ball.

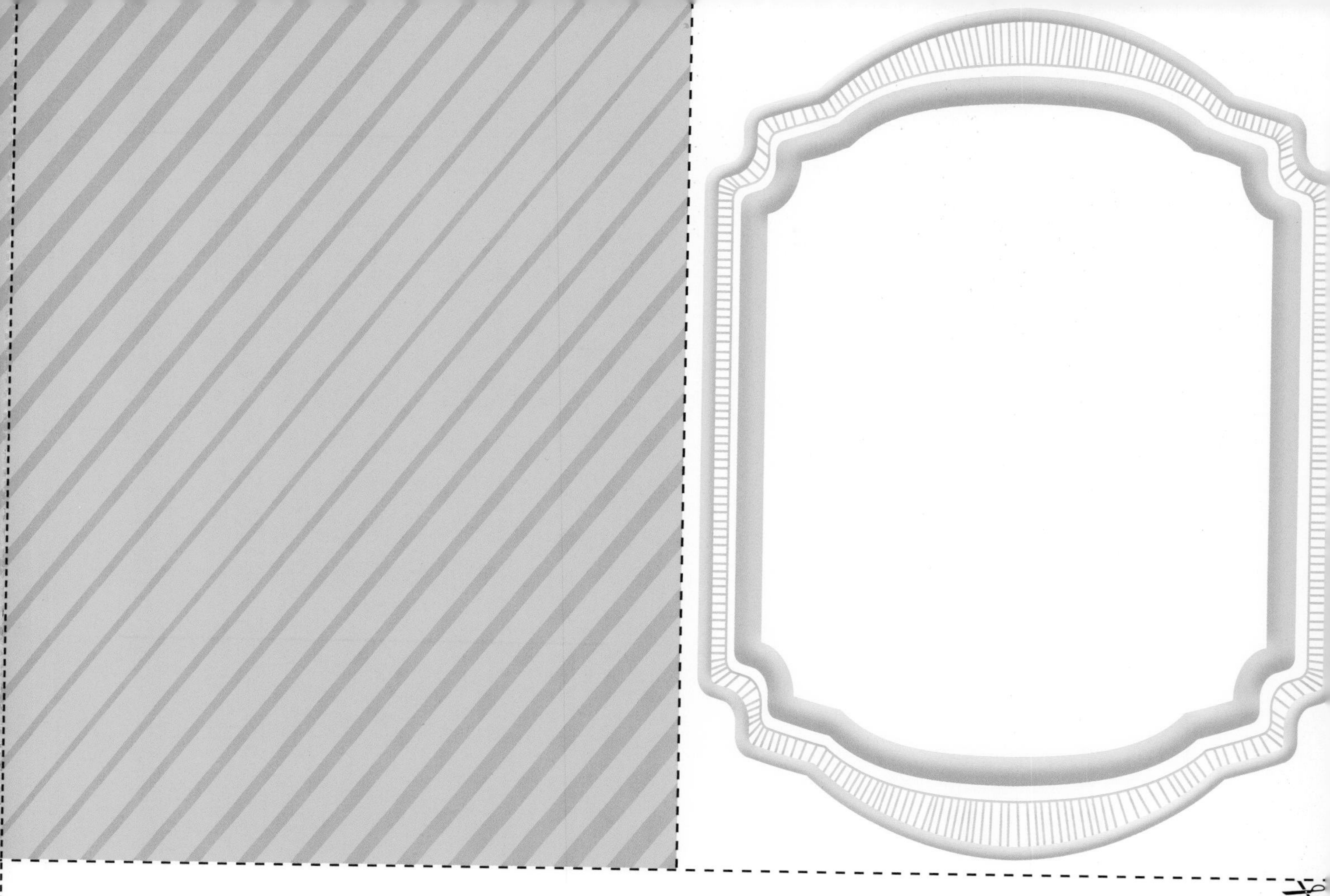

CREDITS

PHOTOS: 2 (t) © Peathegee Inc/Blend/Aurora Photos; (mt) © Photo by Studio Bauhaus; (mmt) © Michael H/Getty Images; (mmb) © Light of Peace/Getty Images; (mb) © Kyodo/AP Images; (b) ©Abdulrahman Alhinai; **3** (t) © Annie Griffiths; (mt) © Aurora Photos, USA; (mb) © Yuji Kotani/Getty Images; (b) © Russell Monk/Getty Images; **5** © Peathegee Inc/Blend/Aurora Photos; **6** © LightCapturedByDamian/Shutterstock.com; **7** © Jacob_09/Shutterstock.com; **9** (l) © Roman Samokhin/Shutterstock.com; (m) © Podfoto/Shutterstock.com; (r) © Tetat Uthailert/Shutterstock.com; **10** (tl, tm, tr, tml, tmm, tmr, bml, bmm, bmr) © Cengage Learning, Inc.; (b) © tatianasun/Shutterstock.com; **11** © Photo by Studio Bauhaus; **12** (tl) © Amero/Shutterstock.com; (tml) © NANTa SamRan/Shutterstock.com; (tmml) © Keith Publicover/Shutterstock.com; (tmmr) © creativesunday/Shutterstock.com; (tmr) © kak2s/Shutterstock.com; (tr) © Ljupco Smokovski/Shutterstock.com; (b) © ullstein bild/Getty Images; **13** (pencil) © kak2s/Shutterstock.com; (crayon) © Keith Publicover/Shutterstock.com; (red book) © Amero/Shutterstock.com; (red chair) © valkoinen/Shutterstock.com; (green chair) © NANTa SamRan/Shutterstock.com; (desk) © creativesunday/Shutterstock.com; (pin board/pins) © Joanna Dorota/Shutterstock.com; **14** (t) © Amero/Shutterstock.com; (mt) © kak2s/Shutterstock.com; (ml) © Amero/Shutterstock.com; (mr) © Pshenichka/Shutterstock.com; (mb) © Keith Publicover/Shutterstock.com; (bl) © NANTa SamRan/Shutterstock.com; (br) © valkoinen/Shutterstock.com; **15** (l) © Aksenova Natalya/Shutterstock.com; (m) © Evgeny Karandaev/Shutterstock.com; (r) © S-F/Shutterstock.com; **16** (background) © Feng Li/Getty Images; (tl) © Piotr Malecki/Getty Images; (tr) Greatstock/Alamy Stock Photo; (b) © tatianasun/Shutterstock.com; **17** (tl, mtm) © Amero/Shutterstock.com; (tm, mbl) © kak2s/Shutterstock.com; (tr, br) © Keith Publicover/Shutterstock.com; (mtl, mbm) © NANTa SamRan/Shutterstock.com; (mtr, bm) © creativesunday/Shutterstock.com; (mbr, bl) © Ljupco Smokovski/Shutterstock.com; **19** © Michael H/Getty Images; **20** (tl, mtl, mr) © Mega Pixel/Shutterstock.com; (tml, mtml, mbl © Andrey Lobachev/Shutterstock.com; (tmml, mtmr, mml) © Andrey Osipets/Shutterstock.com; (tmmr, ml, mbmr) © charles taylor/Shutterstock.com; (tmr, mtr, mbr) © Jesus Cervantes/Shutterstock.com; (tr, mmr, mbml) © David W Hughes/Shutterstock.com; (b) © Plan Shoot/Multi-bits/Getty Images; **21** (tl) © Mega Pixel/Shutterstock.com; (tml) © Armari36/Shutterstock.com; (tmr) © Vtldtlm/Shutterstock.com; (tr) © charles taylor/Shutterstock.com; (mtl) © Andrey Lobachev/Shutterstock.com; (mtm) © Tomislav Forgo/Shutterstock.com; (mtr) © HomeStudio/Shutterstock.com; (mbl) © Andrey Osipets/Shutterstock.com; (mbm) © Jesus Cervantes/Shutterstock.com; (mbr) © Amore/Shutterstock.com; (bl) © charles taylor/Shutterstock.com; (br) © David W Hughes/Shutterstock.com; (foreground) © MicroOne/Shutterstock.com (background) © Eshma/Getty Images; **23** (l, m) © Eric Isselee/Shutterstock.com; (r) © Rost-9D/Getty Images; **24** (background) Agencja Fotograficzna Caro/Alamy Stock Photo; (tl, tr, mtl, mtr) © Cengage Learning, Inc.; (mbl) Matthew Mawson/Alamy Stock Photo; (mbm) © Mardzpe/Dreamstime LLC; (mbr) © Serhii Fomin/Dreamstime LLC; (b) © tatianasun/Shutterstock.com; **25** © Light of Peace/Getty Images; **26** (tl) © Siarhei Kelnik / EyeEm/Getty Images; (tml) © Marc Bruxelle/EyeEm/Getty Images; (tmml) © Jon Boyes/Getty Images; (tmmr) Life on white/Alamy Stock Photo; (tmr) © Eric Isselee/Shutterstock.com; (tr) © Praisaeng/Shutterstock.com; (mtl, mtr) © Ewa Studio/Shutterstock.com; (ml) © Bilanol/Shutterstock.com; (mm) © shikheigoh/Getty Images; (bml) © Dmussman/Shutterstock.com; (bmm) © Subbotina Anna/Shutterstock.com; (bl) © anetapics/Shutterstock.com; (bm) © Arno van Dulmen/Shutterstock.com; (br) © Pete Oxford/Minden Pictures, Inc.; **27** (tl) © Stefan Petru Andronache/Shutterstock.com; (tr) © Trevor Fairbank/Shutterstock.com; (mtl) © Kwadrat/Shutterstock.com; (mtm) © Svietlieisha Olena/Shutterstock.com; (mtr) © Irka Smorodina/Shutterstock.com; (mbl) © absolutimages/Shutterstock.com; (mbm) Zoonar GmbH/Alamy Stock Photo; (mbr) © oksana2010/Shutterstock.com; (b) © MaxyM/Shutterstock.com; **28** © Potapov Alexander/Shutterstock.com; **29** (l) © lozas/Shutterstock.com; (m) © Yuri_Arcurs/Getty Images; (r) Nature in Stock/Alamy Stock Photo; **30** (background) © Steve Byland/Shutterstock.com; (tl) © mariait/Shutterstock.com; (tml) © Wendy M. Simmons/Shutterstock.com; (tmr) © romansu/Shutterstock.com; (tr) © StockShots/Shutterstock.com; (b) © tatianasun/Shutterstock.com; **31** (tl) © Hurst Photo/Shutterstock.com; (tm) © Mega Pixel/Shutterstock.com; (tr) Yulia Chupina/Alamy Stock Photo; (mtl) © Creative Crop/Getty Images; (mtm, mtr) © Super Prin/Shutterstock.com; (mbl, bl) © Eric Isselee/Shutterstock.com; (mbm) © photomaster/Shutterstock.com; (mbr) © Abramova Kseniya/Shutterstock.com; (bm) © ESB Professional/Shutterstock.com; (br) © cs333/Shutterstock.com; **33** © Kyodo/AP Images; **34** (tl, mm) © Stockforlife/Shutterstock.com; (tml, bl) © Dani Vincek/Shutterstock.com; (tm, bm) © Svitlana-ua/Shutterstock.com; (tmr, ml) © Evgeny Karandaev/Shutterstock.com; (tr, mbm) © Jiri Hera/Shutterstock.com; (mtl, mbl) © SOMMAI/Shutterstock.com; (mtr) © Pavlo Loushkin/Shutterstock.com; (br) JOHN BRACEGIRDLE/Alamy Stock Photo; **35** (tl) © Stockforlife/Shutterstock.com; (tr) © Dani Vincek/Shutterstock.com; (ml) © Pavlo Loushkin/Shutterstock.com; (mr) © Svitlana-ua/Shutterstock.com; (bl) © SOMMAI/Shutterstock.com; (bm) © Jiri Hera/Shutterstock.com; (br) © Evgeny Karandaev/Shutterstock.com; (background) © KREUS/Shutterstock.com; **37** (l) © TATSUHIKO SAWADA/Getty Images; (m) © Katrina Leigh/Shutterstock.com; (r) © Coffeemill/Shutterstock.com; **38** (background) © opicobello/Shutterstock.com; (tl, tm, tr) © Cengage Learning, Inc.; (mbl) © MaxxiGo/Shutterstock.com; (mml) © XiaosKitchen; (mmml) © Dinhngochung/Dreamstime LLC; (mmmr)

Dear ____________,

I like English.

Thank you!

Your student,

____

© Stef Hoffer/Shutterstock.com; (mmr) © Vittorio Caramazza/Shutterstock.com; (mr) © successo images/Shutterstock.com; (b) © tatianasun/Shutterstock.com; **39** © Abdulrahman Alhinai; **40** (tl, mml) © ESB Professional/Shutterstock.com; (tml, mmr) Blend Images/Alamy Stock Photo; (tmml, mmml) © Images By Tang Ming Tung/Getty Images; (tmmr, ml) © Imgorthand/Getty Images; (tmr, mmmr) © John-Patrick Morarescu/Getty Images; (tr, mr) © recep-bg/Getty Images; (b) © Cynthia Herrick; **41** (tl) © Robert Niedring/Getty Images; (tr) © Hero Images/Getty Images; (ml) © Regreto/Shutterstock.com; (mr) © SW Productions/Getty Images; (bl) © SCHAMIN/Shutterstock.com; (br) © kali9/Getty Images; (foreground) © wattana/Shutterstock.com; (background) © jakkapan/Shutterstock.com; **43** (l) © exopixel/Shutterstock.com; (m) color to go/Alamy Stock Photo; (r) © Steve Satushek/Getty Images; **44** (background) © Artur Debat/Getty Images; (tl, tr, mtl, mtr) © Cengage Learning, Inc.; (mbl) © Rhiane Alegre-Johnes; (mbm) © Sky News/Film Image Partner/Getty Images; (mbr) © SWEviL/Shutterstock.com; (b) © tatianasun/Shutterstock.com; **45** (tl) © SCHAMIN/Shutterstock.com; (tm) © Gamzova Olga/Shutterstock.com; (tr) © Victoria Blackie/Getty Images; (mtl) © EvgeniiAnd/Shutterstock.com; (mtm) © Artem Malov/Shutterstock.com; (mtr) © Stuart Minzey/Getty Images; (mrl) Westend61 GmbH/Alamy Stock Photo; (mbm) © MaraZe/Shutterstock.com; (mbr) © baibaz/Shutterstock.com; (bl) © Jim Franco/Getty Images; (bm) © Lisa Wiltse/Getty Images; (br) © Digital Vision./Getty Images; **47** © Annie Griffiths; **48** (all) © Hill Street Studios/Blend Images/Getty Images; **49** © Apostrophe/Shutterstock.com; **51** (l) © Paul Orr/Shutterstock.com; (ml) © taa22/Shutterstock.com; (mr) © EllenSmile/Shutterstock.com; (r) © Thai Yuan Lim / EyeEm/Getty Images; **52** (tl, mtl, mmtl, mmbl, b) © Cengage Learning, Inc.; (tm) © Yurara Ohno; (tr) © Tracy and Jessica Tran; (mtm) © Safia Youssfi; (mmtm) © Rhiane Alegre-Johnes; (mmbm) © Juan Leonardo Solari; (mb) © tatianasun/Shutterstock.com; **53** © Aurora Photos, USA; **54** © Subajogu/iStock Editorial/Getty Images; **55** © Art Stocker/Shutterstock.com; **57** (l) © pasha66/Getty Images; (ml) © Neirfy/Shutterstock.com; (mr) © Lawrence Manning/Getty Images; (r) © Odua Images/Shutterstock.com; **58** (background) © Isa Fernandez Fernandez/Shutterstock.com; (tl, tr) © Cengage Learning, Inc.; (m) © Nicescene/Shutterstock.com; (b) © tatianasun/Shutterstock.com; **59** © vs148/Shutterstock.com; **61** © Yuji Kotani/Getty Images; **62** (tl, mtl, mbmml) © fotosaga/Shutterstock.com; (tml, mtmr) © TerraceStudio/Shutterstock.com; (tmml, mtml, mbl) © John Kasawa/Shutterstock.com; (tmmml, mtmml, mbr) © BABYFRUITY/iStock/Getty Images; (tmmmr, mbml) © DenisProduction.com/Shutterstock.com; (tmmr, mtmmr, mbmr) © Magdalena Wielobob/Shutterstock.com; (tmr, mbmmr) © popovaphoto/iStock/Getty Images; (tr, mtr) © Irina Rogova/Shutterstock.com; (b) © Richard Nebesky/Robert Harding; **63** © elic/Shutterstock.com; **65** (tl, bl) © Alex Staroseltsev/Shutterstock.com; (tr, bml) © Nemova Oksana/Shutterstock.com; (bmr) © AlexLMX/Shutterstock.com; (br) © zcw/Shutterstock.com; **66** (background) © sbw18/Shutterstock.com; (tl, tm, tr, mtl, mtr, mbl, mbml, mbm, mbmr, mbr)) © Cengage Learning, Inc.; (b) © tatianasun/Shutterstock.com; **67** © Russell Monk/Getty Images; **68** (tl) © goce/istock/Getty Images; (tml) © LWA/Stephen Welstead/Getty Images; (tmr, mbml) © Domino/Getty Images; (tr, mbm) © Alejandro Iborra Ventura/Getty Images; (mtl, mbmr) © Ariel Skelley/DigitalVision/Getty Images; (mtml) © Jeff Greenough/Blend Images/Getty Images; (mtmr, mbr) © Clover No.7 Photography/Moment/Getty Images; (mtr, mbl) © Samuel Micut/Shutterstock.com; (b) © hadynyah/Getty Images; **69** (tl) © BorneoJC James/Shutterstock.com; (tm) © goce/Getty Images; (tr) © Clover No.7 Photography/Getty Images; (mt) © Samuel Micut/Shutterstock.com; (mbl) © LWA/Stephen Welstead/Getty Images; (mbm) © Domino/Getty Images; (mbr) © Ariel Skelley/Getty Images; (bl) © Alejandro Iborra Ventura/Getty Images; (bm) © MamiGibbs/Getty Images; (br) © D Waljaw/Shutterstock.com; (background) © nito/Shutterstock.com; **70** (tl) © Hayati Kayhan/Shutterstock.com; (tr, mtr, bl) © Kellis/Shutterstock.com; (mtl) © eurobanks/Shutterstock.com; (mbl) © Joseph Jacobs/Shutterstock.com; (mbr) © photo one/Shutterstock.com; (br) © Lim Yong Hian/Shutterstock.com; **71** (l) © Joanna Dorota/Shutterstock.com; (r) © trabantos/Shutterstock.com; **72** (background) © Wayne Eastep/Getty Images; (tl, mtl, ml, mbl) © Cengage Learning, Inc.; (mbml) © sunweitao/Getty Images; (mbmr) © technotr/Getty Images; (mbr) © haizon/Getty Images; (b) © tatianasun/Shutterstock.com; **73** (tl) © Amero/Shutterstock.com; (tml) © Keith Publicover/Shutterstock.com; (tmr) © charles taylor/Shutterstock.com; (tr) © David W Hughes/Shutterstock.com; (bl) © Eric Isselee/Shutterstock.com; (bml) © Marc Bruxelle / EyeEm/Getty Images; (bmr) © TerraceStudio/Shutterstock.com; (br) © John Kasawa/Shutterstock.com.

ILLUSTRATIONS: All mascot artwork created by Fabiana Faiallo; **6, 7, 8, 9, 22, 23, 38, 52, 66, 70, 71** Holli Conger/Maggie Byer Sprinzeles; **10, 75, 76** Andre Ceolin/MB Artists; **14, 15, 24, 36, 37, 50, 51, 79, 80** Barbara Vagnozzi/Advocate Art; **16, 77, 78** Fabiana Faiallo; **28, 29** Constanze Von Kitzing/CATuguea; **42, 43** Kathryn Mitter/Maggie Byer Sprinzeles; **49, 63** Jannie Ho/MB Artists; **56, 57** Jomike Tejido/MB Artists; **59, 69** Jim Steck; **64, 65** Mike Wesley/Painted Words; **81, 82** Gustavo Mazoli/Beehive; **83, 84** Angel Chang/Lemonade; **85, 86** Mike Wesley/Painted Words; **87, 88** Victoria Assanelli/The Organisation; **89, 90** Nomar Perez/Painted Words; **91, 92** Arthur Lin/Shannon; **93, 94** Sahar Kober/Shannon.